For Mom & Dad,
who were there through all of this.

Table of Contents

Part 2: Parenting

Part 3: Seasonal

Part 4: Soapbox Time

Part 5: Short Stories

Conclusion

Inspirational

Prologue

If there is one thing I have learned in my forty-seven years on this earth, it is how little I know. I had once believed that, with age came answers. I suppose, to a degree, that's true. But with each answer we find more questions, and the questions get harder the older we get.

There are two reasons, I believe, why this happens. The first reason is that all of our questions in life revolve around the world as we know it. When we are five years old, our world is still very much unknown; we question a great many things. We wonder why it takes so long for Christmas to come, and why Mommy wants us to eat all of our peas and stop picking on our little brother. Yes, there are times when a five-year-olds' questions are hard ones. Answering the question of 'Why did Grandma have to die?' can break an adult's heart, as can the dreaded, 'Why doesn't Daddy live here anymore?' But these questions are really quite simple at their core. The five year old wants to know why they are hurting. At that age, we are trusting, and we believe what we are told. When we get older, we realize that embracing the 'easy' answers that come our way is often simpler (and perhaps even wiser) than holding out for the truth.

There is another reason why questions get harder as we get older. Questions are compounded with time. Every question we ask, and subsequently answer, leads to more questions. This is not the same as a young child asking his/her perpetual string of 'whys.'

"Why do I have to pick up my toys?"

"Because we asked you to."

"Why?"

"Because they shouldn't be lying around on the floor."

"Why?"

"Because someone could trip over them."

"Why?"

No, the questions that come into our lives at the age of forty-seven are very different indeed; they are the hard questions. "Why can't I quit smoking, no matter how hard I try?" or "Why should I send my son off to fight in a war that I feel is wrong?" In later life, when we ask questions and attempt to answer them, it goes something like this:

"Why does it have to be Jenny who has cancer? She's a wonderful, caring person–why can't it be someone else?"

"Like who?"

*"I don't know! Why should it be **anyone**? Why does God let this happen?"*

"I can't answer that; sometimes, we just have to have faith. We can't know God's plans; we simply have to believe."

"But how can God be so cruel? I thought He was supposed to be a 'loving' God."

"God isn't cruel; we question His plans because we're hurting; but someday, if we keep the faith, we will understand."

*"I don't want to understand **someday**–someday isn't good enough! He healed the blind man, and the lepers; why can't He heal Jenny? Doesn't He care?"*

Obviously, even though we are faced with these questions, life marches on. The answers come and go, and are often forgotten, or they are replaced by new and more pressing issues. At this stage of our lives, it would be nice to be able to go back to that time when we were only asking why we had to pick up our toys. It would be nice to once again be content with the notion that, in time, all of the answers would come. But at forty-seven and beyond, that's no longer good enough. We want the answers *yesterday*, and we often battle the feeling that time may be running out.

Thus it is that I found myself facing my midlife crisis. In my personal, desperate search for answers and a purpose to life, I chose to try to better myself; I returned to school. For several years, I studied, and wrote papers, and commuted to classes. Eventually, I received my Masters of Science Degree in Management and Organizational Behavior. I now know from experience that there is truth in the saying, "It's never too late to learn." And, I also know that, if there is one advantage to returning to school 'later in life', it is that you bring a lot of real-world experience to the classroom with you. You see the underlying purpose of the instructors' questions, and you know the answers they are hoping to hear. But, this 'real-world' experience can be a bad thing as well.

2

Having worked in several manufacturing settings over the course of my life, I can tell you first-hand what the 'real world' is like when working 'in the trenches'. I also know, beyond a shadow of a doubt, that what is being taught about 'business' in the classroom can be a far cry from what is happening in the industrial parks of small-town America. Because classes focus on teaching students how to succeed, lessons are based on how a business *should* be run, which is often not very realistic. While textbooks are full of examples of their existence, cases of real, level-five leadership–examples of business owners and managers who motivate and encourage their workers from the heart–are the exception, not the rule. My experience has taught me that, more often than not, business managers are more focused on their own success and ego than on the success of the business. These managers view employees as an expendable commodity to be used to boost profits. That's a very sober statement, but I have found it to be true.

With this negative view of business, you might be wondering why I chose to study it. I didn't choose to, at least not originally. Before obtaining my Masters of Science Degree in Management, I spent several months enrolled in what Silver Lake College called its 'Transition to Teaching' program. You see, I never really wanted to study business; I wanted to be a high school English teacher. Now that, given my love of writing, made sense. But that, like many other plans in my life, was not meant to be. I discovered (only after studying my way through half of the program) that there was a required certification step that I couldn't complete. In Wisconsin (and perhaps in other states as well), in order to become a licensed teacher you have to complete a process called 'student teaching.' To do this, you have to teach in a classroom setting for six months under the guidance of a 'real' teacher. You receive no income during this period; instead, you pay tuition to make it all happen.

Needless to say, most people over the age of forty have mortgages, car payments and a family depending on them for all of life's little necessities. Alas, I couldn't afford to live six months without an income, and my 'factory job' didn't allow me to 'teach' during the day and 'work' at night. Also, to make matters even more impossible, the 'student teaching' had to be completed in a school that had a student population that was at least a one-third minority. I live in northeast Wisconsin. At that time, the closest school that met such a requirement was over a hundred miles away. All of this forced me to

3

take a hard look at my ability to complete the 'Transition to Teaching' program. Reluctantly, I transferred into the business program and eventually graduated in 2007.

Although academically disconnected, the 'business' program and the 'education' program had their similarities. They both revolved around classes that depicted what life would be like in a *perfect* world. In the 'Transition to Teaching' program, would-be teachers were expected to bring creativity and energy into the classroom. Curriculum would always be written and delivered to meet the different learning styles of each and every student. Also, assessment of each student's knowledge would be custom-designed, so that no matter what the student's learning style might have been–or what level of knowledge they may have had upon entering the class–you could accurately depict that, indeed, each student had learned the intended course work.

This emphasis on individual accomplishment was also present in the business program. Classes I attended stressed the fact that managers should always realize that employees were their greatest asset–and that investing in that asset (through training and fair compensation) was the surest way of guaranteeing the success of their companies. Employees were to be treated fairly, and each was to be recognized and rewarded for a job well done.

But forgive me, for I have digressed; and this book is not about college curriculums, or business, or education–it is about life. This isn't a perfect world, as some classrooms hope to depict. It never will be–especially for those people (like me) who are facing a mid-life crisis! Still, that doesn't mean that life is hopeless. Far from it! Every day, each of us has countless opportunities to change our view of life, and to make the world a better place. This is actually easier to do than you might think. It's not done by changing things around you, though; it's done by changing yourself.

Dr. Phil McGraw has shared many priceless tidbits of advice with the world through both his books and his numerous television appearances. One of my favorite quotes by this life strategist is, "There is no reality; there is only perception." If that's true (and I believe it is), then changing something is as easy as changing the way we look at it. Over the course of a couple years, I submitted weekly stories to a small, local newspaper. The subject matter of my articles varied with the passing seasons, and was often influenced by where I was at in life at the time the article was written. My goal was to take

4

ordinary, everyday things and look at them from a unique point of view. I knew I couldn't change the world–not by myself; but I could change the way I looked at it, and so can you.

With that in mind, I have collected my essays, blown the dust off the pages, and arranged them here. I won't pretend to offer answers to your life's deepest questions; I'm not qualified for that level of analysis. But I can certainly offer questions that you would have never thought of on your own. For example, have you ever wondered, "What does deer hunting in northeast Wisconsin have to do with bright-orange, vinyl-covered recliners?", or "How come chocolate-chip cookies and willpower really can't coexist?" Pondering these questions can absolutely change your perception. Who knows, maybe together we can even change the world. It can't hurt to try.

Organization and Genetics

My mother is a very organized person. For example, all of her bills are stored in a small drawer in her kitchen. On the appropriate dates, she pulls them out, pays each one, and files the receipts away in their designated folders. The folders are then stored alphabetically in a filing cabinet, which is located in an equally organized office.

But that's just a start. Her organizational powers go far beyond simple paperwork. Her bath towels are folded and arranged by color. To open her bathroom cupboard is to be greeted by neat, symmetrical stacks of green, brown and white. I don't doubt that she rotates each stack, so that the towels at the bottom of each pile get used just as often as the ones resting closer to the top.

This is not to say that her house is immaculate, but it's definitely organized. For example, on any given day you can walk in and find stacks of items sitting on her kitchen countertop–but you can also bet each little pile is another example of organization. One is outgoing mail, another is a collection of items she wants Dad to look at, and there's almost always a separate pile for each of her grown children, just waiting for the owner to stop by and claim it. There could be paperwork for my brother, dishes and gadgets she'll be giving to my grown daughters the next time she sees them, and a TV schedule from the Sunday paper (along with several pieces of a decadent dessert!) she's been saving for me.

Even the *inside* of her cupboard is organized. She owns an old set of dishes that came in an assortment of four different colors. To peer into her cupboard is to see alternating rows of yellow, white, blue and pink. The layers do not vary, nor is the order of color allowed to change. In other words, the blue plate will never get to know the yellow one–unless they meet in the sink amidst the bubbles. These layers of color also serve as a security measure. My mother knows at a glance when one dish is missing because the layers are disrupted. When that happens, she scowls at me and says, "Kathy, do you still have that plate I sent the apple crisp over on–you know, the pink one?" Just like that, I'm busted.

It isn't fair. Oh, I don't mind that she knows when I don't return her dishes. What bothers me is that she didn't give me her organizational gene. She gave me her short gene–and the one for gray hair. In a lot of ways, I'm her little carbon copy, but not when it comes to being organized. The paperwork in *my* house tends to live wherever it wants to. Yes, there are stacks of it on my countertop–similar to what my mother has–but mine are organized in a more *chronological* order, as in Tuesday's mail is plopped down six inches over from the pile I got last Friday–and don't even ask me where Monday's mail went. I'll find it when I get the chance.

As for my towels, well . . . they're not folded and organized by color. Normally, they're not even folded. But I *have* noticed the green ones tend to inch their way over toward the same side of the basket where the yellow ones are huddled. Personally, I think they do it for intimidation reasons, not because they have an unspoken desire to remain unorganized. And my dishes? Okay, I admit it. I do stack them in a certain order. But for me, it's a ritual–a sort of celebration. It's my way of announcing to the world, "Hey look, quick! They're all in the cupboard, and in order–and they're actually clean!"

Too Much Junk

I have too much junk. No, let's be totally honest. I have *way* too much junk! I'm am equal opportunity junk collector; every room in my house has its share. In the kitchen, it's dishes. For instance, I have everyday plates in the cupboard, and decorative plates on the wall, and various antique plates resting on yet another shelf. My cupboards are full of pots, and pans, and all sorts of domestic gadgets. There is a pair of pressure cookers, one large, one small, a wire rack for cooling baked goods (last used in 1989?), and a waffle iron that's been tucked away for so long that it would need a formal introduction to Aunt Jemima before cozying up to that bottle of syrup. Of course, I also have items that I *do* use on a daily basis. My 'everyday' plates are easily accessible–they're on the shelf just above the dinnerware set I got for Christmas two years ago (they're the ones that have yet to experience food, or take a bath with Palmolive dish soap!)

My living room is much the same. There are books on a shelf (that I'll never read), magazines that are waiting to be recycled, and a cabinet with 'stitchery' kits that will still be waiting for me when my grandchildren have children. The windowsills are all covered with plants; either that, or there are tipped-over plants on the carpet and a cat in the window where the plants used to be. Of course, there's the usual television set and VCR, but they don't get used very much. Without cable service, the only channels I should get are 2, 5, 11, and 14. I say *should* because channel 2 never comes in, 11 only makes an appearance on a good day, and channel 14 doesn't come in at all–which leaves channel 5. Luckily, all of my favorite shows are on channel 5–or are they my favorite shows because I never get to see anything else?

Under the bathroom sink is an army of cleaners that once promised to make my life easier. As of today, I'm still waiting for them to make their move. They were supposed to remove soap scum, dissolve hard water deposits, clean glass, disinfect the toilet, and leave the air smelling like a fresh, spring day. Lucky for me, I can open my windows and get that last benefit (and for a lot less than I paid for the cleaners!)

Alas, the clutter doesn't stop there, either. In my closet are clothes that I will never wear. There are the outfits I bought for that 'special' occasion. I must have felt pretty in them 'once upon a time,' but that time is gone. And of course, there are the outfits that I will definitely wear again–once I drop those twenty pounds. How much simpler my life would be if I cleared them all out! Then I could take the stacks of clothing that I *do* wear, which are now piled on the top of the dresser, and I could put them away!

Why do I hold onto these things, as though they were treasures in disguise? And I don't mean just the clothes–I mean all of this stuff! Why is it so hard for me to let it all go?

I want to simplify my life, I really do. Perhaps it's finally time for me to deal with all this clutter; it's been years in the making, but I think I'm finally ready to let it all go. How nice it will be to have a house–and a life–that contains only the bare essentials. After all, there's no stability to be found in hoarding dishes and clothes. Even I, the 'die-hard clutter queen', have come to the realization that I'm fooling myself if I believe that I'll need these items someday. There is no someday–only today; and, for the sake of today, it's time to clear them all out. I know; I'll put it on my weekend list of 'Things I Must Do.' It will be like putting my house on a diet. Right now, there's just too much to love!

But, I'm Tired!

I believe that all people can be divided into one of two groups. Those groups are not determined by skin color, gender, nationality, or even age. The difference is far simpler than that, and it is a difference that is so engrained in us that there is no hope for change–no chance of being reformed. You are born, draw a breath, and instantly become one of two things–a morning person or a night owl. It is that simple.

Think about it; you know which one you are. If you're a morning person, you're up at 5 a.m.–even on your days off. Discussing this habit with a night person is guaranteed to bring a look of shock, especially if you finish the sentence with, "I just couldn't sleep." Morning people are the ones who brew the coffee across America–and then offer it to the night owls, who groan and roll over to face the wall. Morning people pick up the newspapers, fry the eggs and bacon, bring in the cat, let out the dog, and whistle the whole while they are in motion; which forces the night owls to groan again and place pillows over their heads. Morning people need to be reminded that you really shouldn't mow the lawn before 8 a.m. on a Sunday . . . especially if you live in town. Perhaps we should make that 11 a.m.–or better yet, noon.

If you're a night owl, nothing a morning person does will make any sense. You'll find the ability to greet the morning in a chipper, wide-awake manner to be a total mystery. Your day begins about three or four in the afternoon. Oh, you might be up and to work hours before that, but you're really not awake. Night owls have a wonderful, automatic-pilot feature that enables them to function, and possibly even be somewhat productive, long before they're really ready to start their day. When evening arrives, night owls are ready to paint the town at about the same time that morning people are settling back in their easy chairs, pulling up the footrest, and reaching for the remote.

Because of mankind's awesome ability to adapt, what type of person you are may have nothing to do with your job or what shift you work. A morning person, stuck in a second shift job, will probably still be up at 5 a.m. ("I just couldn't sleep!"), but will simply be stifling yawns from 7 p.m. on. On the other hand, a night owl, forced to rise early, will be lying in bed at 10 p.m., staring at the ceiling in the darkness, trying to suppress the urge to scrub the kitchen floor because they really have to try and get some shut eye!

I suppose the real mystery lies not in how we survive in a world with people who are our exact opposites, but in why we tend to marry them! Perhaps the divorce rate could be substantially lowered if we simply married only within our own group. It's not that difficult. Picture this: we could all wear colored armbands that designated which type of person we are, thereby eliminating any doubt. Maybe the morning people should have their own side of town, where swingin' hot spots were open and started swingin' as early as 3 p.m., enabling them to have a 'night on the town' that still allowed them to be in bed by eight. On the 'night owl' side of town, all businesses would remain closed until at least noon, and restaurants would serve breakfast until 5 p.m. Yes, I think that should about do it.

Except, of course, for the lawnmower issue. At least wait until the dew is off . . . longer on Sunday. God might be a 'night owl', too. There's no sense in taking any chances.

Brown Paper Sacks and Rainy Days

There is undeniable wisdom in saving for a rainy day. When I was growing up, my parents never had a lot of money to tuck away in a savings account. Their 'savings' fell under the category of 'waste not, want not', which meant that there were always brown, paper, grocery bags stacked neatly in the bottom cupboard, and familiar empty coffee cans serving time in the pantry with everything *but* coffee inside.

In a way, my mother was a recycling pioneer. She never threw away anything that had an ounce of usefulness left to it. Table scraps were fed to the animals; empty baby food jars stored dried melon seeds, waiting to be planted the following summer; and wrapping paper that had somehow miraculously survived Santa's magic touch–and our overly-eager fingers– was refolded and stored away for yet another Christmas. Of course, there was never any guarantee that the salvaged paper could be located when the following December finally arrived, but it was still strangely comforting to know it was there . . . somewhere.

I was all grown up and on my own before recycling finally caught on. While that concept was a little different than the one my mother lived by, I found myself embracing the idea of recycling with open arms. It made sense. It *is* wrong to be wasteful. Besides, recycling finally gave me a use for all of those brown, paper bags that I was now stashing in the bottom of *my* cupboard. My mother would agree–the apple never falls far from the tree–and then she would make sauce out of it. In spite of (or maybe because of) my mother's style of recycling, the house I grew up in was always orderly. We were never without, and I remember 'getting by' to be a creative endeavor. But it was that art of saving something for a rainy day that I never quite got past.

Last Christmas, my mother gave me an assortment of practical gifts (wrapped in neatly folded, slightly familiar paper), one of which was a hair dryer. It had 1800 watts of professional power–the ultimate styling tool–or at least, that's what the box said. And still says. I see it every time I open the bathroom cupboard to stack the towels or retrieve some soap. You see, I never felt the need to take it out of its box; after all, my old hair dryer works just fine. Oh sure, the power switch occasionally sticks, and the words "off", "low", and "on" have long since disappeared from the handle's smooth plastic, but all in all–with little more than an occasional rap on the side of the sink–it dries hair just fine. So I'm saving the new one for a 'rainy day.' That should be the perfect time for a new hair dryer, if and when it comes.

A thought occurred to me the other day. Maybe I should let my mother know that I still have it. After all, hair dryers are pretty practical–and Christmas and birthdays are always just around that proverbial bend. And, while I'm on the topic with her, perhaps I could drop a hint or two for one of those new-fangled racks that install in your cupboard and organize all of the shopping bags that are hiding there. Even better, I should just ask her for a simple, signed proclamation that states, in black and white, "The rainy day is at hand!" What a wonderful gift–freedom at last.

Growing Old

I try not to wear shorts in public. Call it vanity, if you like, but I call it common sense. I don't feel I should show the whole world something I don't even care to look at myself. Too many years of factory work (standing countless hours) on concrete floors, have taken their toll. Add to that the fact that I was born with a bad hip, which means my 'good' leg has had to pull double duty while the 'bad' one just tags along for the ride. I think you get the picture. And it's not pretty.

While I'm certainly not crazy about the way my legs look, I try to view it as the personal price I must pay to walk this earth for an extended period of time. Varicose veins, stiff joints, gray and/or thinning hair, a need for eyeglasses–they are all tolls we must pay to 'take the ride' we call life. Oh, there are some alternatives and 'fixes'; a few, at least. Hair color, plastic surgery, contact lenses, they all help us look younger–at least for a while. The only thing on that list that I could afford is the hair color. I was tempted once to try it. Just once. For about five minutes. That was how long it took me to decide that I didn't need another 'project' added to my list of 'things that must be done on a regular basis'. Besides, I figure God probably knew what He was doing when He gave me this hair. And, if the gray strands seem to be taking over, I know for a fact that I've earned them–each and every one.

So what if I'm getting older? I'm not alone; it's happening to all of us. My mother was at a seminar several years back, and the main speaker talked of how wonderful it would be if life were reversed. We'd all start out old and wrinkled, and eventually end up as infants. She didn't remember all of the details of the presentation, but somehow we all finished up in this world as just a twinkle in someone's eye.

I've pondered that idea for a long time, but its logic escaped me. But, now that I'm forty, I'm beginning to understand. We'd start out old and tired, but with a good idea of what life was supposed to be about. As time went on, the aches and pains would fade. We'd be able to move faster and get more things done. We could stay awake for longer periods, and we'd no longer desire that nap that has become part of our daily routine. After years of working and feeling better all the time, we'd suddenly be teenagers and all the answers would again be ours. We'd stay out late, sleep in late, and leave the bills to someone who was older than   (and not as wise as) us.

About the time we got tired of this lifestyle, we'd learn the joys of catching fireflies in mason jars and running through puddles after a summer shower. We wouldn't care where our meals came from, and would no longer see the logic behind cleaning off our plates. The 'older' we'd get, the more wonder would surround us. How do butterflies fly? What makes a rainbow? Does Santa really know when we're sleeping? And can you guess what the best part of this stage of our lives would be? It's this—we'd constantly be surrounded by people who loved us, and cared for us, and made us feel special.

It all sounds pretty good. Too bad it doesn't work that way. That's okay, though, because we can still learn to age gracefully; we can do it with class. But, as for wearing shorts in public, sorry—that's just not for me. Call it vanity, if you must. I just figure there's enough tragedy in this world without me wearing shorts.

So Many Choices

It's no wonder that we're so tired; we have far too many things to do and choices to make on a daily basis. It starts every morning with the alarm clock and our first of many choices; do you want to wake to music or a buzzer? You jump in the shower and ask yourself, 'Do I have time for conditioner today?', or 'When was the last time I shaved my legs?' This is followed by, 'Do I really want to shave them *now*?' You get dressed for the day and wonder if you should dress for comfort, or for style. A truly wise person has clothes that belong in both categories at the same time.

The ride to work is a continuation of choices. Do you listen to whatever the radio has to offer, or do you slide in a CD or cassette? Perhaps you have an audio book along for the ride. Do you listen to it now, or save it for the long ride up north this weekend? Should you stop for gas before or after you've put in your hours at work? (If you wait until *after*, the price will have no doubt gone up and you'll end up paying more!) And what about groceries? Better wait until after work for a food stop, because choices abound in that store. Whole milk or 2%? Margarine or butter? Frosted Flakes or Fruity Pebbles? Generic toilet paper or Scott tissue–which one has more 'wipes' for your money?

What will you have for supper? Do you want to cook healthy, or is today one of those days when calories don't count? Will there be coffee with your meal? Of course there will, but will it be regular or decaf? And let's not forget about dessert, or will you choose to pass on that?

What will you watch on TV tonight? Do you have cable, and if so, does having it make the choices easier? What do you allow the kids to watch–educational programs or the Cartoon Network–or will you choose to leave the television off and have a family game night instead? What game will you play? Perhaps, after that, you could curl up with a good book. Again, you must choose. What book will you read?

Then, when payday finally comes, you're faced with the *important* choices. Which bills do you deal with and which ones get shuffled back into the pile? Can you afford to put some of the check into savings? Can you afford not to? If you do opt to save some, how much should you save? The bank statement came on Monday. Will you sacrifice some of your free time this weekend to attempt to balance it once again, or will you choose to let it go for just a bit longer? Are you still thinking about that dream job–the one you're going to go after someday? If so, is this the week to tackle that résumé–or will you opt against change and stay where you're comfortable?

And what about the 'big' choices, the ones that will affect the rest of your life? You know which ones I'm talking about. Do you go out with that guy who's been calling for weeks? And, if you do go out and you do 'hit it off', do you let him move in before saying "I do"? Do you move to another town, do you have another child? These questions are certainly important, but thankfully they don't come every day. They don't have to. We have our hands full with the little choices; but then, it's the little choices, made time and again, that really make up the bulk of our lives.

Still, there is one easy choice that will actually simplify your life, though few people actually make it. The choice is this–you can choose not to worry. I know; it's not as easy as it sounds, but it's not impossible. Worry can be so overwhelming, and it serves no purpose. I read somewhere that there are only two things in life we worry about–things we have control over, and things we don't. If we have no control over something, it's out of our hands and it really makes no sense for us to worry. If we *have* control, there are things we should be doing to fix the problem–so it still makes no sense to worry. Simple, isn't it? You make hundreds of choices every day. Choosing not to worry is one of the smarter ones you can make. You choose.

New and Improved?

I bought my son his birthday present last night. He's turning fifteen and loves to download music from the internet. The problem, as he tells it, is that all of the songs are locked in his computer and he can't take them with him when he's out and about. Solution? Modern technology is a wonderful thing. I ran to Green Bay and, for an outrageous fee, bought a tiny device that measures 1"x3". It's called a Nomad MuVu. It plugs directly into a port at the back of the computer and, with the help of an installation CD, pulls the music files out of the computer and stores them for travel in its 64MB of memory. Using the tiny earphones provided with the unit, my son can now take his music everywhere and listen to it for as long as he likes–or at least until the batteries run down.

It's amazing, it really is. This tiny piece of technology that resembles a miniature garage door opener has as much memory space as my entire first computer had, which was a Commodore 64. It is also much easier to dust! On the down side, it is very apt to get lost if my son isn't careful. It weighs less than an ounce (without the battery installed) and will play up to twelve hours on a single charge. It's also supposed to be incredibly easy to use. The box states that you just drag and drop your MP3s/WMAs and other files straight onto the Nomad MuVu (why does that sound like I'm speaking a foreign language?) and you're set to go. Of course, *I* don't understand any of that (and I wouldn't know an MP3 or a WMA if it walked up and bit me), but, that's okay because my son understands it and the gift is, after all, for him.

But oh, how times have changed. I remember my most favorite birthday gift. It was the year I turned seven. As a little girl, I stumbled out of bed and found the neatest Tonka truck waiting for me at the breakfast table. (Yes, I said *truck*. I never had much use for dolls.) It was a lime-green safari vehicle, and the back end was fitted with a cap that carried different types of animals, each in its own little stall. The stalls were fitted with plastic grates that swung up and out, releasing the animal held captive inside. I played with that gift for countless hours, freeing the animals to roam around the house or yard, than gathering them up and securing them in their cages once again. That truck put on a lot of miles. It frequented the sandbox outside when the weather was nice, and occupied my playroom indoors for many years to come.

Eventually, the cages wore out and the animals' legs got bent and broken. Yet, even after that, the truck survived. I think my younger sister eventually inherited it. She would rest one foot on it and propel herself around the house, riding it like it was a skateboard. (Tonka trucks were built tough–there's no doubt about it!) Today, even though that birthday morning was a long time ago, I remember the thrill of unwrapping that present like it was yesterday; that's how special it was.

Does the MuVu compare? I doubt it. It's more expensive, a lot less durable, and not nearly as "user friendly." I'll bet it will get lost and forgotten a lot sooner, too. Maybe that's because there's really nothing imaginative about it. It stores and plays music. It doesn't take you on safaris, or allow you to envision far away lands. Oh yes, I know music can transport you, too. Music has its own magic. But the MuVu will pass, as all technology does; tomorrow it will be replaced with something even smaller and better. My son will not remember it in twenty years–not the same way I remember my Tonka truck and the little animals arranged in their cages, just begging to come out and play.

Labels

Humans use labels to describe people and situations in our lives. It simplifies things. You can "eat like a bird", "run like the wind", or be "as cunning as a fox". Of course, over the years the meanings of some labels have changed. For example, at one time it was a very positive thing to be considered "gay", and if you were "straight" back then, it meant you upheld the law and walked the straight and narrow. Today, if someone was "as honest as the day is long", I suppose it wouldn't mean very much, as quickly as the days fly by. And the labels "cute as a cucumber" or "cute as a bug's ear", where did those come from? The world may never know.

The labels we assign to things also tend to lack accuracy. We are apt to say that someone who eats very little, or picks at their food, "eats like a bird." In truth, birds have voracious appetites and spend a great deal of their lives in search of, and eating, whatever they can. When we accuse someone of being "sloppy as a pig", we should consider that pigs, if given a choice, prefer being clean; they only wallow in mud to stay cool and to find relief from pesky insects. In addition to this, they will answer their 'call of nature' in one corner of their pen, and they thoroughly love sleeping on a clean pile of straw. In a perfect "pig world", all pigs would live in a climate-controlled building, complete with a pest control system, just like you and me.

And, of course, we've all heard about "the old, gray mare" and how she "ain't what she used to be". We've always been made to think that that's a *bad* thing. I beg to differ. Anyone who's spent time around horses will know that's not true. I've owned a few horses over the years–geldings, mares, and ponies. I've owned old horses, young horses, and everything in-between. I even had a young stallion at one time that was extremely spirited, but very sweet. I can say, speaking from experience, that if you want a horse the whole family can use and trust, you buy an old mare. If you want a horse that's calm and settled down, you buy an old mare; and if you're looking for an animal your children can work with and ride, you definitely *don't* buy a pony–you buy an old mare.

I have found the same principle is often true when it comes to people. Have you ever found yourself in a situation where the walls were caving in, the world was collapsing, and everyone was ranting and raving about all the terrible things yet to come? In that moment, did you look around and find your eyes drawn to that one person who remained calm and cool, who refused to jump at the threatening shadows, and ultimately brought the group back under control? You know the individual I'm talking about. For every fear you voiced, she had an answer. You swore the world was ending, and she said it wasn't so. After a while, you started to believe her, because she seemed so calm and so sure. That, my friends, is the old, gray mare. She's seen it all, done it all, and been through it all; you can set off firecrackers under the broad expanse of her belly and she won't even flinch.

I draw strength from these people. I admire their calm way of handling the unknown, and their quiet strength that can so easily be mistaken for lack of concern. Say what you want about them, they are blessings in disguise. They know what's important, and–more importantly–what's not. They've seen, heard, and done it all. While others are panicking and racing about, the old mares stand firm, 'settled in the traces', and continue to pull their weight. I don't know about you, but I could use a few more "old, gray mares" in my life. In fact, I'd love to be just like them–calm and secure. Heck, I've already got the 'graying' part right, how hard can the rest of it be?

The Fair

I took my son to the Oconto County Youth Fair on Friday night. Chris wanted to see Wes Harrison perform in the Grand Stand, and I wanted to try and spend a little quality time with a child who was growing up way too fast in a world that was moving far too quickly.

I attended this fair as a middle-age, one-time 4-H member; one who had exhibited projects at the fair in ages long past. As it had been years since I'd attended, it was a melancholy surprise to find the fair smaller than I remembered it to be. They'd added a new cattle barn and made a few other what I viewed to be 'drastic' changes, so everything looked slightly strange and a little out of place. There weren't nearly as many rides as there had been when I was a child, or maybe things just loom larger in memory than they had been. They didn't even have a Scrambler, which surprised me; but they did have our favorite ride–the Tilt-O-Whirl!

For those of you who aren't familiar with this ride, it consists of several round 'cages' that can spin in either direction. This ride doesn't leave the ground, as many do. Instead, as the cages travel around their circular path, they move over a series of hills and valleys. How quickly the riders spin in their individual cages depends upon what direction you lean as you travel over hills. If you lean into the down-slope, you spin very quickly and the momentum forces you back in your seat. If your timing is off, however, the slope becomes a hill and you remain frozen in position. It's one of those rides that is different every time you get on. Sometimes you can't get the thing to twirl no matter what you do; at other times, you are spinning so quickly that you can't hold your head forward and you're plastered against the metal mesh that forms the backrest behind you.

With tickets priced at $.75 (and four tickets required to get on), I told Chris we only had time for one quick ride on the Tilt-O-Whirl before we had to head to the grandstand. After all, we didn't want to be late for Wes Harrison's six o'clock show. There were no lines at the rides, so we handed the man our tickets and climbed aboard. The Tilt-O-Whirl began to move, gained speed, and seemed to go on forever–spinning and twirling, rising and dipping. We laughed, and whirled, and shouted to each other, "Left! Right! Right! Left! No, no–right!" as we tried to anticipate which way the ride would spin, and in what direction we should lean in order to get it to *really* twirl! When the ride finally ended, we got off and wobbled away, breathless from laughing so hard. Somehow, we made our way over to the show, dizzy and queasy, and very much grateful that we hadn't just eaten.

Wes Harrison, also known as Mr. Sound Effects, was as funny as we remembered him to be from a previous show we'd seen at Wisconsin Dells. After the performance, he sold copies of his tapes and CDs, so we purchased one and asked Wes to autograph the jacket. The cost of the CD was $10. We really didn't need it; we already owned the cassette version. But, this was Chris's chance to meet Mr. Harrison, and it's hard to put a price on a child's opportunity to meet someone he's been a fan of for all his young life. All children need heroes, and they come in all shapes and sizes. Here was a man who made his living by being different–by using his unique talent of being able to do numerous different sound effects with no equipment other than his vocal cords and an ordinary stage microphone. Here was someone who had become a success (and made people laugh) simply by being himself. That's a good lesson for anyone, and an even better one for my son, a child who also feels he's just a little different from everyone else.

We left the grandstand, treasured CD in hand, and decided we had time to ride the Tilt-O-Whirl for one last spin. The man wouldn't even take our tickets . . . I guess he felt any forty-something-year-old mother who wanted to ride that thing twice with her son ought to ride for free! After that, Chris played a few carnival games and won a few more 'treasures'. As the man wrapped the small goldfish in a plastic bag and handed it to Chris, I thanked him and we moved on. We walked away and I consciously silenced the familiar voice inside of me. It was a voice that firmly pointed out the fact that I had just thanked someone for handing my son a goldfish we'd spent $7 trying to win, and it was a 'feeder fish' that would have sold in any local pet store for a mere 25 cents.

Still, it didn't matter in the long run–not really. We were at the fair to have fun, and to spend some quality time together. Viewed from that perspective, it wasn't the *fish* that we had paid for–it was the experience. Sure, we could have spent some quality time together at home and saved the money. We could have watched a good movie, played a board game, or even gone for a walk–all for free. But part of the magic of childhood is the memories, and who can argue with the obvious? Once you get past the amount of money spent, memories are still being made at the county fair.

Do You Have a Minute?

My family tells me that I work too much. I suppose I can see their point of view. Indeed, every minute in my endless parade of hectic days is spoken for. One after another, they fly by–a kaleidoscope of changing images. Each new minute brings a fresh challenge, an unseen demand, or a new twist in a schedule that I dare not write in stone, for fear it will change. I have flowers in the garden, but no time to pick them. I have a lovely deck out back, on which I have never sat with a cup of coffee in one hand and a good book in the other. Even if I did find the time to spend in a lawn chair, chances are the bees that hover around that deck would drive me back inside–they're just one more thing on the list that I never seem to get to. Despite getting so much done each and every day, I still have to knock down the hornets' nests, mulch the berry patch, then finish the concrete and fieldstone steps out behind the house . . .

Sometimes I get tired just thinking about it. To make matters worse, I'm a self-employed businessperson. Even as I write this, I am all too aware of the fact that there are boat cushions in my shop, waiting to be upholstered. The gentleman wants them for the weekend and it's already Wednesday night. I work fulltime. I am a mother and a grandmother who has a household to manage and a business to run. Add several pets and an eleven-acre lot to the list, and anyone can see why I'll never catch up.

Still, I tend to find it all fascinating. If I didn't, I'd go crazy. The minute you let a chaotic schedule get to you, you are no longer running your life–it's running you. I have come to realize that I am not busy because I'm the victim of a hectic schedule; I am busy because I choose to be. Okay, maybe it wasn't a conscious choice–at least, not at first. Maybe, in the beginning, I surrounded myself with chores and lists because the work gave me a sense of security. It kept me too busy to ask the questions that tugged at my mind's sleeve–the eternal questions, like 'Why are we here?', 'What is life all about?', or the ultimate question of 'What happens when it's over?' Maybe back then I thought I'd find the answers buried in the work, but I didn't. The only thing that was buried there was me.

Today, I've come to realize that the important questions of life cannot be silenced by busy hands. Even if you shoo the questions away, like pesky sparrows they will return to roost in their familiar places–because they mean to be pondered, and they have to be answered. For the most part, I have found a peace in the chaos that is my life. Mowing my lawn, tilling the garden, working at my job–none of these things brings the answers I am searching for. Yet by doing them–and by being self-disciplined–I have come to know myself a little more. With knowledge, comes peace, and with peace, comes answers. Do I know what life is all about? No, but I have learned to be content with the journey. I believe that I will look up one day and the answers will be there, waiting to be found. Like those familiar sparrows I have shooed away, they'll be resting just over my shoulder. Perhaps they were there all the while, just blending in with the leaves. I had only to believe, and look closer, to see them.

Of Math and Mice

I just finished helping my son with his homework, although I suppose 'helping' might not be the right word. It's more like I offer moral support. He was working on freshman algebra. Needless to say, math has changed a lot since I was in school. We weren't allowed to bring a calculator to class; now, it's a requirement. We had to write out the steps we used to solve every problem. That way, the teacher could check our work and see where we went wrong. My son only writes down the answers in his notebook. His work is done on scratch paper and is seldom collected and checked. His grades are based on how well he does during the quizzes and tests. This class structure seems to work for him; I prefer the more rigid structure of the "good old days".

He was solving a complex problem. "An eagle is perched on a cliff 145 feet above an open field. It sees a mouse. Folding its wings, it dives at its prey at a speed of 118 miles per hour. Approximately how many seconds does the mouse have to escape?" Wow. He's ciphering away and I'm thinking, 'Poor mouse.'

He takes the height of the cliff where the eagle is sitting and its initial speed of descent, then plugs those numbers into something called a quadratic formula. After punching the calculator keys and figuring a few square roots he announces the mouse has about 2.13 seconds until it's toast. Ah, the power of math.

But this is the real world and having had more experience in it than my son has, I have to challenge his announcement.

"Now wait a minute," I say. "The cliff might have been 145 feet high, but what if the eagle flew up a few feet before it dropped? Wouldn't that change the answer?"

"Mom . . ."

"And what about a wind–is there any wind, perhaps an updraft? And if the mouse sees the approaching shadow, wouldn't that lengthen its window of opportunity for escape?"

"I don't believe you're doing this . . ." He rolls his eyes.

"And how much does the eagle weigh? Would a fat one drop faster?" I always have to push it. He's closing his book, leaving me to sit alone at the table and ponder the poor mouse's fate. "How do you know you have the right answer?" I call after him.

"Because the book says so." The door to his room closes and the echo of his remark is all that remains.

The book tells him when he's right. Yes it does; I can't argue with that. I wish all of life–not just algebra class–could be lived by the book. Things would sure be simpler. Besides, something with a name as important sounding as a quadratic formula *has* to be right, whether or not I understand it. What I *do* understand is that my teenage son still enjoys my company. He lets me help him with his schoolwork. That makes me very lucky–a lot luckier than that mouse.

It's Only Paper

Paper is one of the many things in life that we take for granted. In its multiple forms, it surrounds us and makes our lives easier. It is there to accompany us on our journey, from beginning to end.

When we are born, a birth certificate marks our entrance into the world . . . followed by an announcement in the local newspaper, complete with all the details. We grow bigger, and older, and eventually enter school. Suddenly, paper is all around us. There are report cards, art projects, spitballs, and paper airplanes. There are dreaded notes sent home by the teacher, and one or two written excuses sent in by Mom when we missed school due to the flu.

Eventually, we earn a diploma and head out into the world. At this time, the paper in our lives might take the form of 'help wanted' ads, job applications, résumés, and cover letters. Yet, in spite of the need to find employment, not all of the paper in our lives is work-related. There are probably more than a few love letters in there somewhere. These may be followed by a marriage license and wedding invitations. Once married, you need a place to live. You might sign a rental agreement; or perhaps a new home is in your future, so you obtain the proper permits and sign a loan application for that perfect little house, whose floor plans you study and work at revising for months. And all of this, of course, is on paper.

When you get ill, there are prescriptions, written instructions from the doctor, or maybe even a release form you need to sign before going into surgery. This is followed by cheery 'get well' cards and, of course, the not-so-cheery unavoidable bills and confusing insurance forms. At times like this, paper may actually seem to be the enemy.

As if that's not unpleasant enough, paper can also come in the various forms of divorce decrees, court summons, and traffic tickets–even the dreaded job-termination notice, and all of the other monthly bills we will have paid through the course of our lives, have come in the form of paper.

Paper can be a simple grocery list, a 'honey-do' list, or a goal you wanted to set down in writing. It can also carry the words that break or heal a heart. It can be the paper you sign at the veterinarian's office, giving them permission to end the life of a dear pet–and it's the tissues you dab your eyes with during the long ride home. A piece of paper can declare war, or announce peace; it can send our troops off to a faraway land, or it can bring them home to waiting arms. It can outline and map entire cities, or the world. It can be a letter to a friend, or a tiny folded treasure on which you've written a very dear secret. In the very end, it's a death certificate . . . and a place someone jots down the eulogy that you'll never hear.

Paper has helped to shape and mold our lives. It brings us the news and keeps us informed. We hold it in our hands and it is nearly weightless, yet it is strong enough to change the world.

The Tape . . .

The car I'm currently driving is the only vehicle I ever bought brand-new. Before the extended warranty, rust proofing, tax and destination charges were added on, the sticker price was $6995. That was in 1997. Of course, it didn't have electric mirrors, electric windows or electric door locks. It wasn't equipped with air conditioning, an automatic transmission, or the luxury of power steering. It didn't even have a radio in it. Now *that* I had to fix!

One of the first things I did was buy a stereo for it. It was a simple unit with an AM/FM radio and a cassette player. Because the stereo didn't have a CD player, it wasn't exactly a state-of-the-art piece of electronic equipment. That was fine with me. In my mind, it didn't make sense to get a stereo with a CD player for a couple of reasons. Number one, most of my music was already on cassettes. I recorded it myself from my vinyl album collection. Now there's a music collection with some history! But there was another reason why I didn't want a CD player. I got the distinct impression that the shocks in my car were little more than dime-store springs slid over Popsicle sticks. I'll be honest; I'm just not into music that stutters–or worse yet, skips. At least with a tape player, you know what you're getting and you know it's going to work. That's what I thought; that was my logic, until that fateful day when I popped a tape in.

The tape player worked fine–at first. But after a week or two, it developed the tendency to stick in the 'fast forward' mode, which makes John Denver (and any other artist, for that matter) sound very much like a munchkin who somehow managed to get stuffed into a car stereo and was working his way toward the glove box. If the car hadn't been so small, I swear I would have looked for them! I discovered that I could trick the stereo into playing at the correct speed by inserting the tape while the power was off; but eventually, it seemed to get wise to that maneuver. Then I learned that it worked better if it was warm, so I started parking the car in the sun. I abandoned that practice rather quickly. Listen, I really like my music, but when it's 90+ degrees out, even I'm not that dedicated!

So tonight I was headed up to Marinette. The temperature was just right and the stereo seemed to be in a cooperative mood. I felt lucky. I inserted my tape of David Soul and began enjoying the first lines of a song called 'Silver Lady'. Life was good. Then it happened. Silence abruptly filled the little car. That *wasn't* good–not good at all. I jabbed at the eject button with all the force of a Samurai warrior wielding his sword for the kill, and the tape came flying out, it's brown, shiny ribbon trailing behind it like crumpled intestines that were still trapped in the tape player's metal jaws.

In another life, not so long ago, I would have parked the car and pried open the flap on the tape player. Using makeshift tools gathered up from my surroundings (a ballpoint pen, a plastic fork, the amputated arm off a pair of sunglasses), I would have operated to free the tiny hostage. I would have taken extreme care not to damage the tape–ever hopeful that it could be saved. Once released, I would have carefully wound the tape back into the cassette's body, smoothing the ribbon as I did so, preventing kinks and watching for curls. I would have done all that and more–in another life.

I've been told we cannot live in the past. So now, cruising at 60 mph (and ever grateful that my car's four little cylinders could even carry me that fast) I reached down, grabbed the tape and gave it a jerk. From somewhere inside the otherwise silent stereo, there came the sharp snap of something breaking and the cassette was free. The tape which, up until that point, had entertained me for some twenty odd years, slid out of the stereo. It looked like two flimsy, brown tentacles, curled and limp. I tossed the murder victim onto the passenger seat and the wind from the open windows (no air conditioning) tossed the ends of the tape to and fro, as though it were waving goodbye to me, the player, and the world.

When I got to Marinette, I tossed the broken tape into the first garbage container I saw. The action surprised even me. It was something I would not have done last week, maybe not even yesterday. But I am learning; yes I am. You see, in that other life, I would have held onto it. After all, it was the music I listened to when the idea for my first novel wormed its way into my head. It was a tape I'd made back when my daughters were not yet even in school. Now they're grown and gone and have children of their own. That brown, shiny ribbon held songs that could take me back in time . . . back to days spent at college; episodes of 'Starsky and Hutch' on a black & white, small screen TV; and a cramped, musty apartment that felt so much like home. Music can take you back like that–it has the power. But sometimes, just sometimes, there's more power in letting go. That's what I'm learning; that and to never trust that double-crossing tape player again.

On the Road

I work in the small town of Peshtigo, Wisconsin, and live in Oconto, fourteen miles away. It's not a long commute, but my drive takes me down a dangerous, two-lane road that connects the neighboring towns. I should rephrase that; it's really not the road that's dangerous. After all, this is Wisconsin, not Colorado. The road doesn't have hairpin curves, or aging guardrails that separate motorists from rocky, deep ravines. It's not the road that makes my commute dangerous; it's the people.

This is a deadly stretch of highway. Countless accidents–many fatal–happen on this road each year. During my daily commute, I can't count the number of times I've personally witnessed what could have been a serious accident. There are usually two things involved; excessive speed and some stupid driver's desperate need to pass. It doesn't seem to matter how fast you are driving, or how many other vehicles are in front of you or behind you, all going the same speed; some idiot has to come along and try to play leapfrog. It happens all the time. We apply the brakes as someone up the line allows the passing car to merge back into the flow. Oncoming traffic, its path temporarily blocked, has pulled to the side of the road to avoid a collision. We all shake our heads and think, 'There goes another one.'

In eight years, this highway is slated to be expanded to four lanes; but the present road is a typical country highway, with its twists, and turns, and numerous dips. When you drive it everyday, you get to know it pretty well. You drive past the rolling farms, the new houses, and the small businesses just taking hold. You watch as farmers plant their fields and harvest their crops. You notice deer at the edge of the woods, and pastured Holsteins, and you notice the crosses–those simple, wooden structures that mark where a motorist has lost his or her life. There are several along that route, and I know of a few more places where they were never placed but could have been. There are also crosses that have disappeared. Once placed by a grieving family or friend, they've fallen to snowplows, and the elements, and the simple passage of time. Traces of them rest in the overgrown ditches, as all of life marches past unaware.

There is one certain cross, close to Drees Road, that has always caught my eye. It is always tended to, and decorated with adornments that celebrate the changing seasons–flowers in the spring, a wreath at Christmas, a baseball cap for the summer months. One day, when I was driving home, a lady was at the site, tending to the cross. In spite

32

of always being in a hurry and behind on my next task, I pulled into the next driveway, turned around, and went back. I wanted to talk to her; I wanted to hear the story behind the tragic marker. It was a story, I felt, that she also wanted to tell.

The cross, she soon told me, was for her cousin–a young man named Craig. He'd been killed there on a foggy night, just two weeks after his high school graduation. It had happened in 1994. She told me that, to this day, her uncle (the boy's father) still wouldn't drive by the spot. He took another route, miles longer, whenever he needed to get to town.

I listened to her story, and I felt my heart go out to her and her family. She spoke of how Craig had lived two days beyond the accident, and the family had been approached about organ donation. They had consented and, from their tragic loss, five strangers got a new chance at life. Perhaps the sorrow is lessened a bit when some good can come from tragedy, but there is still no replacing that which is gone.

I still drive that road every day. I still notice the crosses, and remember some of the stories. When the highway is widened, it will help; but anyone who believes that adding more lanes will fix this deadly stretch of road is sorely mistaken. North of Peshtigo, and on up to Marinette, the highway has already been widened. Count the crosses placed in that short distance of five or six miles, then convince me that more lanes will save lives.

The only thing that can really save lives is people. We need to slow down; we need to be more courteous. Have you ever had someone speed around you–risking life and limb–only to find them stopped at the first red light in the next town, waiting right in front of you? Was it really worth it; did they get there any quicker? Have you ever been tempted, while the light was still red, to approach their car, rap on their window, and ask them what the hell they thought they were doing?

I don't recommend doing so; it's probably not a good idea. The other driver is obviously in a big hurry and most likely not in a very good mood. We want to believe that people in 'good' moods are courteous–that they're not willing to risk their lives, as well as those of other motorists, just to get somewhere five minutes, or thirty seconds, sooner. But it's something to think about. Slow down, watch out, drive sober–these are the only ways to make our highways safer–no matter how many lanes stretch out in front of us.

Perseverance

There's a lot to be said for 'hangin' in there'. If you're determined enough, you can do just about anything you set your mind to. I've listened to those exact words, time and again, from teachers, self-help manuals, and some very good friends. But lately, I've been hearing it a lot, and the lesson has become a little more personal. You see, I've come to share my home with someone who shows me the meaning of perseverance everyday. His name is Riley, and he's my daughter's cat.

Now, I understand that there are skeptics out there who don't believe you can learn anything from an animal–especially a cat. It's true; our feline companions can be aloof, independent, lazy, obnoxious, stubborn–even a little 'flighty'. Would you believe, some people are actually afraid of cats and are certain that they can't be trusted? If a black cat crosses your path, it's bad luck, and an old wives' tale claims that a cat can steal the breath of a sleeping infant. I can see how these would not be traits that you would look for in an instructor. But then, Riley is not a typical instructor, or a typical cat.

He, my daughter, her husband, her two children, and the balance of her pets, moved in with me almost two months ago. The arrangement has been wonderful–and it is giving me ample ideas to write about in upcoming weeks. You can look forward to articles on, 'What life is really like living with a Martha Stewart Wanna-Be', and 'How to enforce the no-flushing rule when someone else is in the shower.' But for now, let's get back to Riley.

Riley is the embodiment of a spirit that cannot be told 'no'. He is into everything–and I mean *everything*. He is on the table, on the counter, and on the dresser. If you open the dryer, he hops in. If you aren't careful when you go out the door, he darts out between your legs (even though he's never been an outside cat and has no clue what to do when he finally makes it out into the wild unknown). If you're drinking coffee, he checks to make sure it's not too hot; if you're trying to cook, he wants to inspect all the ingredients. If you're doing dishes, he wants to help wash. If you're brushing your teeth, he wants to play with the water as it swirls around the sink. He loves to push plants out of windowsills and canisters off of counter tops. Afterwards, he sprawls out in their spot and looks at you, half closing his eyes, as if to say, "Now, don't I look better here than they did?"

Of course, I try to discourage such behaviors. I've resorted to *trying* to discipline the animal. My daughter and her husband have also tried. We toss him down, he lightly jumps back up. We scold him and he looks at us with that "Who, me?" look of his. We consulted some published pet experts. One suggested using a squirt bottle filled with tepid water to discourage unwanted behavior in cats, but that doesn't work with Riley. This cat loves water; he has even been known to take baths with family members! They toss him out and he jumps back in. If that's not perseverance, I don't know what is!

So, the days go by and Riley continues to do what Riley will do, when and where he wants to do it. He's inspiring; he truly is. How does that old saying go? "If you can't beat 'em, join 'em." Let's all be 'Rileys'. So, with that in mind, don't ever give up. If you really want something, go for it. Move the canisters, chance the wide-open spaces, dare to get wet. Don't worry about being accepted or loved. Riley doesn't, and yet he is. People are funny that way. We don't have to impress the ones who truly love us. They will love us just the same, no matter what crazy things we may try to do. In fact, just like our Riley, they may even love us a little more.

Aging

Do you remember the day you turned 'old'? Was it the first time the grocery clerk called you 'ma'am'–or was it the first time you went into a tavern, ordered a drink, and didn't get carded? Do you remember when you stopped looking for the end of the rainbow, or stopped making wishes on falling stars (because you had so many things to wish for that, by the time you narrowed the choice down, the star was gone)? Do you remember when it was springtime, and you floated withered leaves or small twigs in the rushing currents of the melting snow and watched them disappear–tiny vessels en route to a world where dragons were real and magic made all things possible? Do you remember simply believing?

And when was the last time you did something silly? When was the last time you tried to catch a snowflake on your tongue, or laid down and made a snow angel in a wide open spot–like right, smack dab in the middle of your yard? Sometime this last summer, did you pick a mature dandelion and blow away the seeds, then loop the stem together to make a bracelet for your arm? Did you spray yourself or a friend with the garden hose; or walk barefoot through a puddle just to feel the mud between your toes; or catch a frog just to feel its cool, clammy skin?

When, exactly, was the moment when we all grew up? Don't get me wrong, I'm not looking to place blame. It wasn't our fault; we had to do it. There was no escape. The job, the house, the bills, a family–they all demanded that we grow up, face the facts, and pull our heads on straight. After all, it's hard to appear mature and responsible when we're looking in the mirror to see what color our Blow Pop Sucker has turned our tongue–especially the blue raspberry ones! As our mothers all told us, on numerous occasions, "Would you please just act your age!"

So here we are now, all grown up. We sigh more than we laugh. We worry more than we wonder. We manage the household, and pay the bills, and laugh at the foolishness of anything 'make believe'. Despite this, we flock to theaters and bookstores to experience a good story–to lose ourselves in a fantasy, if only for a while. A good movie or book appeases the child within us. It's a permissible magic, a safe 'make-believe'.

It doesn't have to be this way. We don't have to miss out on all of the fun. My challenge to you is to do something silly–and do it today.

Eat a handful of snow (without pondering what you've *really* just put in your mouth!) Have chocolate milk on your breakfast cereal. Buy a box of Cracker Jacks and dig for the prize. Who cares if it's just a piece of junk–enjoy the thrill of the chase! If you go shopping and find yourself in a parking lot with a hill, get a good running start and step up on the cart for a ride! No hill? You can push yourself along with one foot! No fair looking to see who might be watching; let them get their own cart and take their own ride!

Do something that makes you happy today–something that brings a giggle to the surface, something that makes you feel young again. No one said that the magic had to disappear; no one said that we had to stop believing. There are enough shopping carts, and Blow Pops, and Cracker Jack prizes to go around; you've just got to be willing to grab your share. Besides, why should the kids be the ones who have all the fun?

What Time is Dinner?

I was raised in a home where the days were very structured. While there were always surprises when you operated a dairy farm, there were no surprises when it came to our daily meal schedule. We had breakfast at seven, dinner at noon, and supper at a quarter to five–precisely at a quarter to five. The cows, it would seem, did not like to be kept waiting, and milking time followed the evening meal. Because we needed to be in the barn and beginning the evening chores at 5:30 sharp, our supper was at 4:45. No exceptions. And we ate fast.

Of all the children in my family, this schedule affected me the most. It gave me just enough time to get off the school bus, change my clothes, and feed the cows their silage and grain before I could even *think* about feeding myself. When (and only when) I was done with this first set of chores did I get to sit down at the supper table. When our meal was finished, the table was cleared and my older sister (who was the *inside* girl in our family–cows were yucky!) did the dishes, while I headed back out to the barn. By half past five, Mom and I had fired up the vacuum pump that ran the milking units and we were set to tackle the evening chores. The only thing that ever altered this schedule was a rare power outage, during which we'd sit around, feeling slightly disoriented. We'd stare at the walls, or each other, asking, 'What does a person do at this time of the day if you can't milk cows?'

It's been about ten years since my parents retired from farming and the cows were all sold, but my mother still adheres to the same meal schedule with an almost religious fervor. This predictability makes it extremely easy to 'mooch' a meal off of her, as you know exactly what time to 'just happen to show up.' Those who know my mother understand the irresistible appeal of eating at her house. There's never been a better cook born. Ever.

I am not like my mother in this aspect; cooking is not one of my strong points; and the afore-mentioned tactic of 'simply showing up' to mooch a meal would never work at my house, as I'm not very good at schedules, either. In my house (with only one child left at home), it doesn't seem to matter too much if the meal times vary an hour either way. Show up hungry at my door, and chances are you'll end up fending for yourself, no matter what time it is.

Which brings me back to the purpose of this article: 'What time is dinner, anyway?' I think I was almost thirty when it was brought to my attention that not everyone eats 'dinner' at the same time, and some people never eat 'supper' at all. They eat breakfast, *lunch* and dinner. What's up with that? Where did supper go? 'Lunch' in my childhood home was the snack I begged off my parents just before I went to bed–usually a bowl of kettle-popped popcorn, or a handful of chips. Considering this evidence, it's easy to see why I was a tad bit confused by this bit of news.

When my grown daughters came for a visit this past weekend, I discovered my son-in-law was a member of the 'breakfast/lunch/dinner' group. In an effort to show him the error of his ways, I got out the World Book Dictionary and proceeded to look up definitions of various meals–I'm a real fun hostess, let me tell you! But my research only left us more confused. Here's what we discovered:

We started by looking up 'supper'. My 1990 dictionary defines it as "the evening meal; meal eaten early in the evening if dinner is near noon, or late in the evening if dinner is at six or later." *Dinner* at six or later–and another meal to follow? Wow! That led me to look up the definition of 'dinner' to see what time *it* should be served. Again what we found was of little help. According to the dictionary, 'dinner' is "the main meal of the day. On weekdays, dinner is usually eaten in the evening. A Sunday dinner is usually eaten in the afternoon. *In the city we have dinner at night, but in the country we have dinner at noon.*" Our confusion was now total and quite complete. Dropping down a few entries to 'dinner hour' didn't offer much help either, as the dinner hour is simply defined as "any particular time when people usually eat dinner', and 'dinnertime' is the time at which dinner is served." So there you have it, whatever it is.

I don't think I was very successful at convincing my son-in-law that he'd been eating the wrong meals at the wrong time of day for his entire life. That's understandable; old habits die hard, and no one really listens to their mother-in-law anyway. All I know is that Jesus must have been raised by a mother a lot like mine. After all, he gathered his disciples for the 'Last Supper', and that pretty much says it all.

Deer Hunting from a Recliner

Reif Road is one of the many small back roads situated between my house and the town of Peshtigo. On occasion, when I want to take a more scenic route to work, I will take County W to Reif Road, which then brings me out to U.S. Highway 41. When it isn't winter (and the deer are behaving themselves), it's a nice drive through some rural scenery. There are barns and pastures, corn fields and forests–all of the things you'd expect to see during a drive through northeastern Wisconsin. There are also a few things you wouldn't expect to see.

On the north side of Reif Road, just before it reaches the highway, there's an upholstered recliner sitting in the middle of a hayfield. It found its way out there in time for deer-hunting season in November last year and is still sitting there today. It is now late June; last week they baled hay around it. It's really nothing special, just your average recliner. Driving by, you cannot see if it is equipped with any out-of-the-ordinary hunting paraphernalia–no heat-seeking missile launcher or high-tech radar. (Laugh all you want–we Wisconsinites take our deer hunting seriously!)

No, this chair is just what it appears to be–a ratty, old, brown recliner that once blended in nicely with the dying vegetation of November. I'm thinking that maybe it was even chosen for the job from some 'old-chair retirement home' due to the fact that its fabric was camouflaged to fit the hunting season. I can say this with some authority, because its predecessor (which previously occupied the same spot in the field for a year or so), was upholstered in a hunter-orange vinyl. Whoever placed this chair out there was serious about fitting in with the requirements of the hunting season!

Once I got over the initial shock of seeing a chair in the middle of an alfalfa field, I began to speculate on the advantages of hunting white-tailed deer from this position. Such a hunter would have a clear view of the open field around him, a comfortable seat on which to wait, and (if things got a little slow) he could kick back and catch twenty winks. Okay, I'm being just a little sarcastic, but once my amusement wore off I found that I was still struggling to understand the *real* reason the chair was there. What *really* inspired someone to put living room furniture in the middle of a hayfield?

Eventually, I came to the only conclusion that made any sense. I reasoned that the chair had been placed there for an elderly man to use; someone who was no longer able to make his way around in the woods, but was not yet ready to give up the thrill of the hunt. This was, of course, pure speculation; but it seemed logical enough. Some elderly hunters sit on hay wagons, some in converted ice-fishing shanties–this one preferred a La-Z-Boy. It was the only explanation that made any sense.

Someone else, having accepted such an explanation, would have dropped the topic and moved on to ponder another of life's mysteries. However, being the creative soul that I am, I just couldn't quite let it go. What would it be like, I wondered, to be a recliner and suddenly find yourself sitting in the middle of a field? Would you feel liberated, or abandoned and angry at being left exposed to the elements? Would you miss the Seinfeld reruns and the sound of human chatter?

No one can really say, but I have come to realize that there are some correlations between that chair and life. In many ways, we are like that recliner, sitting all alone in the middle of a field. Think about it; how many times have you found yourself someplace you were never meant to be? In shock or anger, you might have looked around and said, "How in the *&#@ did I get here?" You might have even called out in the stillness–just one quiet voice in the middle of a vast field–and perhaps it seemed like there was no one around to answer.

Sometimes, that's just the way it is. One of the great, exciting (and scary) things about life is that it comes with no guarantees. We have worries, doubts, anxieties–and the grass is always greener on the other side. From our perspective, some other people seem to have it all: no worries, a successful career, a loving family. They appear to live in a 'comfort zone.' As we see it, their problems are small, their bills are few, and all the choices they make seem to come out right. We may even envy them; they are living the life that we want to live.

But appearances can be deceiving. Their lives may be no less chaotic or confused than ours; we just fail to see what's really in their 'hayfield'. Who is to say what lies around the corner for any of us? How can we know what fate has in store? If we are wise, we hold onto our faith, and trust in the future. We live our lives with the belief that we won't be offloaded and left in the middle of a hayfield . . . yet accept the fact that it may well happen. And, as for that old recliner on Reif Road, there is a bright side to its fate. True, it's been abandoned. Sure, it sits alone. But how many recliners have seen so many sunrises, or felt the breezes stir across their seats? Yes, it sits out in the rain, but how else could it have ever learned about rainbows?

The Stone Walk

Last weekend I finished my stone walk. It took me eight bags of Portland cement, countless Red-Ryder wagonloads of gravel, a pile of fieldstones from along a neighbor's fence line, and two shovel handles to complete. All these items, and two years of time, combined to produce a fieldstone walk that meanders downhill from my house all the way to the garden. (Side-note: I completed the entire project by mixing the cement by hand in a large metal tub; so, if anyone needs a caldron-stirring witch for Halloween this year, I think I could definitely qualify!)

It's a nice walk, and I think I'll like it even better when it doesn't look so fresh and new. I'm planning on planting daffodils alongside of it to welcome the spring, and I'll probably add an assortment of perennials and annuals in the years to come. But for right now, it's pretty much done.

It's a good feeling to finish a project, especially one that takes a lot more time than you figured on spending. I can still remember the day I took the can of spray paint and marked the grass where I wanted the walk to go. As I have since told my mother, had I known it was going to turn out to be so much work, I probably would have changed my mind and abandoned the project before it was even begun. I would have opted to erase the lines by mowing over them; that would have been so much easier. But no, I had to be stubborn (I mean, determined!).

The good thing, of course, is that the project is complete. I am through playing with concrete, at least for now. No doubt next year I'll start a new project; after all, there are one and a half bags of Portland cement still sitting in the garage. What I don't use for traction on the ice this winter will be calling to me next spring–begging to be mixed and formed into something. No, I'm not crazy; it's just that mixing concrete and placing rocks in it appeals to some part of me. If I spend a few days (or years) constructing a project like my walk, I know it will always be there. Every time I look out my window or stroll through my yard, I will enjoy the fruits of my labor. If I'd spent the same amount of time cleaning the house, I know it would still be messy. Some jobs just seem to come undone; they reverse themselves when no one is looking. I think little gremlins must come in while I'm sleeping and undo all my best efforts! Okay, maybe I am a *little* crazy, opting to stir cement with a shovel as opposed to using a broom to clean my kitchen floor, but the main thing is that the walk is done.

And what a walk it is! I think one of the things I find most appealing about it is that each stone is unique. They all feature different shapes and colors. In fact, the only two things they have in common are that they have one smooth side to step on, and concrete now binds them all together. It struck me as I was playing with the grey, sloppy mixture–placing each stone randomly in the hardening ribbon–that the walk I was making was a lot like life. The stones could represent different events that we experience, different troubles we have to overcome, and the concrete represents our energy–our faith–that binds it all together. It is only at the end, when the entire 'walk' is finished, that we can look back and really see what we've accomplished. It is only then that we know how far we have come, and how each individual 'stone' has led us on our way.

Details

I have no doubt that details are important. For instance, if you're following a recipe, they can mean the difference between creating a fantastic dish or dealing with a week's worth of leftovers that no one wants to eat. If you're taking a trip and you forget some of the details of the directions you were using to get there, you will probably end up lost. Remembering to tie your shoes is an important detail. So is brushing your teeth. And, when it comes to filing your income taxes, details can be the deciding factor in whether you're heading for a refund or an audit.

Still, at some point details can be overwhelming and we have to see past them. If left unchecked, details can even start running your life. It is the curse of modern days; we have become so efficient at managing our lives that we rise to the challenge of trying to stuff as many details as we can into every single day. Sure, squeezing five errands in between leaving work and picking the kids up from school can be considered admirable. It's a real thrill to see how much you can cram into a brief 45 (or even 20) minutes. But the errands are only details and, if we look past them, we come to realize that we have too much to do and not enough time in which to get it done. In one sense, I suppose that focusing on the 'details' perhaps saves us from seeing a truth we'd rather avoid.

Let's be honest. Most of life is details. Where we work, how much money we earn, what kind of house we live in–we are raised in a society that judges us on just such details. Worse yet, we judge ourselves in the same way. Oh, I won't argue that a better job and more pay wouldn't make life easier or more comfortable. However, I will argue that (more often than not), the more money we make, the more we spend; so we really don't end up any better off. Sure, we may drive a nicer car or live in a bigger house, but that just means that, if we die tomorrow, our kids will have more "details" to sort through and divide. Will having these things have made us happier? I'm betting not.

I'll be the first to admit it; as I get older, I get fussier about the details in my life. But for me, the details are sunsets, uncensored laughter, and treasured moments of hard-won self-worth. When the circumstances of my life annoy or anger me, I lessen the tension and the stress by asking myself a simple question. "If I live to be a hundred and I am looking back on my life, will this crisis (whatever it may be at the moment) even matter?" I have yet to run up against a situation where the answer to that question was 'yes'. In fact, I have developed the tendency to not worry or stress about anything that will no longer be important in ten (let alone one hundred) years.

Details. They are everywhere. Trying to corral or control them will drive you crazy. Instead, figure out what *really* matters in your life, then push the rest aside. Details are spectacular if you're trying to paint a landscape; but, when it comes to life, they may well spoil the big picture.

Downtime

I hate the downtimes. Those are the times when nothing seems worth the effort, the times when you're pretty much ready to admit defeat, the times when you want to look up to heaven and say, "Alright already, I think I've had enough." I guess downtimes are all part of being human, and I try to rationalize my way through them. I tell myself that I wouldn't appreciate the good times if there were no bad ones for contrast. I try to be adamant in assuring myself that every cloud has a silver lining; and of course, there is always the realization that so many other people are worse off than I am. But, in the end, I'm not very good at reassuring myself.

I often find myself questioning what it is that I am doing with my life, here in this moment. Call it a mid-life crisis, or call it insanity, there are times when I just don't understand the 'big picture'–any of it. During such times, I deeply question everything about life as I know it. For example: if humans evolved from apes (as evolutionists believe), then I believe we have come an awfully long way to get to the mess we're in today. As smart as we are, we still can't find a way to feed all the people. It seems something humans invented (called 'politics') gets in the way. Murderers run loose in our streets and honest people lock their doors to attain the illusion of safety. We pollute the earth, take up too much space, and can't seem to understand that there are benefits to being kind to one another. On the other hand, if we were created in God's image and aren't 'mutated monkeys', then He's got to be plenty disappointed in us. We don't put Him first in our lives. There are bills to pay, yards to tend, and committees to serve on. Some of us give Him whatever time is left; still others give Him nothing at all.

All these things and more run through my mind when I'm feeling down, and I see myself (a tiny speck in the grand scheme) and I have to ask, "What difference could I possibly make?" If I should live to a ripe old age and look back, what is it that will catch my eye–my fine house with a manicured yard and a paved driveway, where someone else now lives? Will I look back on a career that took up too much time and energy? Will I remember the times that I laughed and cried? I should hope the last choice would prove to be true. And I should hope that I've laughed 'with' others a thousand times more than I've laughed 'at' them. And I should hope I'd have laughed at myself most of all. As for the tears, perhaps they're really a sign of hope; for when we care enough to hurt and to cry, then we haven't hardened our hearts too overly much. As long as we can cry, we can be there for each other–and hold out hope that others will be there for us.

Such is my analysis of the downtimes. They pass, as all things do. We may even forget they ever existed. Not every day can be good, not every friend will prove to be true. And yes, every cloud may have a silver lining, but that doesn't mean it won't bring some rain.

Angels

I believe that angels exist; but, contrary to popular belief, they are not invisible, winged creatures who protect us from temptation. They are not silent and ethereal, and are not always beautiful. In fact, they come in all shapes and sizes. They are living, breathing beings who surround us on every side. All we have to do is open our eyes and hearts, and they are there.

Look for them. Break down the barriers. Hold out your hands and you will find them. They are hidden in our neighbors, in our co-workers, and in our friends. They are disguised as many things–a receptionist who makes us feel truly welcome, a stranger who holds the door when our arms are full of packages, the driver of the car who holds up traffic so we can merge and get in. Angels don't have to be celestial–angels are those souls who touch our hearts and lighten our loads. They go that extra mile, or step, to help someone out. They make us smile, make us feel worthwhile; they put us first and themselves second.

Last week I had car trouble and I suddenly seemed to be surrounded by angels. Call it idiotic, if you want, but they were angels to me. The first one pushed my little car around a parking lot at work so I could pop the clutch and get her started. The next one wiggled the right wires a few hours later so I could drive her home *without* having to get pushed and pop the clutch again (which, by the way, is soooo embarrassing.) Another angel answered his phone early on Saturday morning and talked me through how to fix the car, even when no stores in the area could get me the right part. Maybe you're thinking those are all just little things, but that's the magic of angels. Without even being asked, they do 'little' things that mean so much more to the person on the receiving end. Angels are what they are–helpful, compassionate people who don't live by the motto of "me first."

So . . . here's the challenge. It's your turn. Once a day, be an angel. Let someone know they're worthwhile. Hold a door, send a long overdue card, say an encouraging word, let someone else cut in line ahead of you . . . The possibilities are endless. For example, consider that grouchy check-out clerk. I dare you to get her to smile. Say something nice (and sincere!). You can do it. Will it be easy? Probably not, but it will definitely be worthwhile. Try it once and see how it feels.

I am grateful everyday for the angels I encounter. I embrace them as friends, or as passing souls, whichever they may be. To the ones who stepped forward last week, I thank you. But then, angels don't do what they do for gratitude. They do it just because. So the next time you see an opportunity to help out, or to lighten someone's load, don't ask, "Why should I?" Instead ask, "Why not?"

Strange Race of People

We truly are a strange race of people. We pay membership dues at local health clubs for the privilege of using the workout equipment and indoor running track, then fight over the closest parking space at the mall, as though a walk of one hundred feet or more will kill us. We order the ultimate burger combos at our favorite fast food restaurants–complete with fries and a secret sauce–then wash it down with a diet soda in an effort to appease the health gods. We read self-help books by the score in an effort to better know who we really are, yet a stranger often greets us when we look in the mirror. Even those of us who claim to have found our 'true selves' still labor forty or more hours a week at a job that has nothing to do with who we are or what we want to accomplish in the set span of our lifetimes. We hurt those we claim to love; we wander aimlessly with no goals and openly wonder why we never 'arrive'; we lose patience and are overly critical with our one greatest asset–ourselves. We preach of compassion and love, yet leave puppies by the roadside in garbage bags to die. We are indeed a strange race.

Imagine turning on the evening news and not seeing the news at all, but a detailed lifeline–your own. Imagine flipping through the channels and finding the same image at every stop. Imagine. There before you would be the answers to every question imaginable. When you were born, rode your first bicycle, stumbled upon your first broken heart, did your very greatest deed . . . and died. Died. There's the date, in black and white. No more guessing how many years are out in front of you, no more fooling yourself about immortality, no more avoiding the issue. There it is. What would you do if the date fell in the next month, the next year, decade, twenty-four hours? What would you do?

It's scary to realize that there is only a set amount of time left to do all of the things your heart desires. No doubt, many of us would chastise ourselves for having wasted so much valuable time in the pursuit of what–money, prestige, a better job, a larger car, simple recognition? To have our lifeline laid out before us would no doubt cause a great deal of anguish, torment, and soul searching, because we'd no longer be able to live under the guise of having an infinite supply of tomorrows to accomplish our heart's desire. The lucky people will see that lifeline and know what they should do with the remaining time. The truly blessed people, however, will have been doing exactly that all along.

The Horse's Secret

I have always loved horses. As a young girl, I got lost in every horse story I could get my hands on: *The Black Stallion, Black Beauty,* and the entire *Misty* series. *My Friend Flicka* was the first novel I ever read. I thought that having a horse was the greatest thing I could wish for. And then I got one.

I now know the truth about owning horses–and about the mixed blessing of getting what you wish for. I discovered that horses are a lot of work and require a lot of money to maintain. They demand a great deal of time, and it's really best to know all you can about both training and working with horses *before* you get one. Of course, I didn't know all of that back then, but I do now. And I've learned something else about horses, too. I now know what it is about them that captures my heart; for me, they symbolize the very best way to live life. It may sound crazy to even consider patterning one's own life after that of a horse, but let me explain.

The magic of horses–good horses–is that they are a splendid combination of power, humility and discipline. Visit any local horse show on a summer afternoon. The horse that ends up in the winner's circle is the one that floats gracefully around the ring, with its neck arched and its tail streaming behind it. The animal appears to be self-directed, aware of what is expected of it, and willing to complete the task. The rider does not struggle to control the animal; he doesn't drive his heels into the horse's side to make it move, or haul back on the reins when he wants the animal to stop. He doesn't shout, and holler, and whistle at the animal like we see in all the old western movies. Instead, the pair–horse and rider–moves as one, in perfect unison. The rider, the master, guides the animal, and the horse responds with grace and power. The horse trusts his master, and the master earns that trust.

The challenge for us is to live life like that horse. Find your Master, nurture your faith, and live to serve both. With true humility and grace, follow the gentle cues of the Master, and thereby find your stride. Serving something does not mean you're weak; practicing humility does not mean you're inferior. If we lived as horses live, we would understand the meaning of work, yet would still frolic when we had the chance. We would be powerful and confident–as magnificent as the horse in the scene from the movie *Braveheart* which William Wallace uses to lead the troops into battle–and yet we would be humble enough to allow ourselves to be led. Being led can be a powerful thing if we can trust ourselves enough to do it. The trick, of course, is to know and trust your Master–the rest is inside your heart.

Doing Dishes

Don't you hate it when you walk into a room and promptly forget what you're there for? Or have you ever poured yourself a cup of coffee, and then wondered where you set it down? Some blame these experiences on forgetfulness and old age, but those aren't the reasons why this happens. In reality, we are simply hapless victims of a series of chained events. Don't believe it? Let me explain.

The scenario, for me at least, goes something like this. One morning, I notice there are a few dishes in the sink, waiting to be washed. I decide I'll tackle them right away, while the day is young; then I'll move on to bigger and better things. As I run the sink full of dish water, the cat reminds me that she has not yet had her breakfast. I cross to the cupboard where I keep the canned goods and open it. While looking for the cat food, my eyes settle on the cans of tomato sauce and tomato paste that are stacked alongside of the Purina 9-Lives. This reminds me that I have to make sloppy joes that morning because my grown children are coming over for the day and will be there in time for lunch. I have an epiphany; I can save time by opening all the day's required canned goods at the same time.

Smiling at my own logic, I snatch the three required cans from the cupboard and cross back to the counter. The opener is ready and waiting. As I am opening the tomato paste, I realize that I forgot to take the hamburger out of the freezer the night before. I cross to the freezer, remove the brick of frozen meat, place it in the microwave, set the appliance on defrost and activate the timer. I turn to cross back to the sink to begin washing the dishes and promptly trip over the cat that is still waiting for the tuna/salmon entree that is now open, but still resting on the counter. I plop the food in her dish and rinse out the can in strainer side of the sink, next to where the dishes are still waiting

Once the container is rinsed, I attempt to toss it into the recycling container that hides in my bottom cupboard, but the container is full. I pull it out, prop it against my hip, and head for the basement, where the items will be systematically sorted into larger barrels to await their trip to the recycling center. On the way to the basement, I pass the laundry room and remember that I had thrown a load of clothes in to wash before retiring the night before. Not wanting them to smell like mildew, I set the recyclable container down and quickly begin to transfer the clothes from the washer to the dryer.

At this point, of course, the phone rings. Hastily, I toss the rest of the items into the dryer, along with a softener sheet, set the dial to 50 minutes, and hit the start button. I then lunge back toward the kitchen, where the phone is now jingling for the third time. Too late, I remember the container of assorted recyclables that I had set down before tending to the clothes. I stumble over it, sending tin cans and plastic bottles scurrying across the laundry room floor. The cat, startled from her breakfast by the commotion, lets out a strangled 'yowl' and streaks toward the living room.

Somehow, I manage to answer the phone just before the answering machine kicks in. It's my daughter calling to tell me that they'll be an hour early. She wants to know why I'm out of breath. I tell her I was doing the dishes. There is a pause. She is wondering what could be so physically demanding about doing dishes that I'd be out of breath. Knowing that my phone is stationed in the kitchen, she chooses her words carefully and asks why it took so long to answer. I laugh it off and tell her I was delayed when I tripped over the recyclables. There is another hesitation on her part. When she finally speaks, there is a definite 'tone' in her voice. She's wondering if her mother is really alright, or if the years are beginning to take their toll. She's a smart girl, though; she wouldn't dream of asking.

We end our conversation and I lightly toss the phone onto the cupboard, right next to the sink, where the dishes are still waiting. The microwave is beeping; the meat should be thawed. From the corner of my eye I see the cat peeking out from behind the couch, one room over. She's wondering if it's safe to finish her tuna/salmon entrée. I assure her it is, then turn my attention back to the sink.

I can picture the scene at my daughter's house. She is hustling her family into the car, anxious to be reassured that 'Grandma' is ok. She should know better; she's been here when I'm having one of 'those' days, or I've misplaced my coffee cup. It's not a pretty sight. So you see, I really don't 'forget' why I go into another room; it's just that twenty more things clamor for my attention along the way, and I try to tackle them all before the journey ends. I'm not getting older, just overwhelmed. I know, I know–I should just be more organized. But, in my own defense, I usually make my day's organizational list as I sit and drink my morning coffee; and, at the moment, I don't know exactly where it is.

Freefalling

I am forty-two years old and freefalling. After seven years with the same employer, they called me into the office and said that they were letting me go. They handed me some standard forms to guide me through the process of filing for unemployment, and provided me with information on continuing my health insurance, if I desired to do so. I was also offered a $3000 severance package, which I would get once I signed the waiver that promised I wouldn't sue them for wrongful termination. That was about it. Oh yes, they wished me luck.

There was no reason given for my termination. The research I did in the days to follow has assured me that employers don't need a reason. Employment, in most cases, is a voluntary thing–on both the employers' and the employees' part–and either one can sever the relationship at will. I had an excellent attendance record, no bad performance reviews, and I had three weeks paid vacation time coming–with another three due in four short months. I guess that, when it's all said and done, it often boils down to the fact that giving 110% on the job may not be enough. But that shouldn't surprise me, not really.

In today's world, they say that 'nothing is like it used to be'. Gone are the days when an employee would start his/her career at a company and retire from that same company somewhere down the line. Small companies are bought out by corporations, and those corporations are run by people who are only interested in the bottom line. To add to the mess, the people who are 'calling the shots and running the show' are often several states and a conference call away. They know nothing about 'their' employees, or how the show is really run. Thus, their decisions are based on numbers and 'total sales for the month'–oh yes, and one other thing, they trust their on-site 'manager' to fill them in on how it's all going.

If that individual is a true manager, he knows his people, and he knows they are the lifeline that holds the company together and keep it running. He understands the human element of working–the bond that develops between workers, the support network that exists, and the sense of camaraderie. He understands that the good workers are the ones who take pride in what they're doing and the role they play in the company's success. But sadly, the on-site manager often has to crunch the numbers to show a profit, thereby saving his own hide. Thus, the axe falls and heads must roll.

So, for me, another painful lesson in life is learned; but, it's not a catastrophe. A child developing a grave illness, forest fires that consume thousands of acres, losing someone you hold dear–those are catastrophes, not this. Is it scary? Yes, it is. Does it take my breath away and cause my heart to race? You bet. But it's not the end of the world–not even close. Is it sad? Yes, more than a little, but perhaps I feel most sorry for the workers I've left behind. I was their supervisor, as well as their friend. They are the ones I guided for seven years, the ones whose jobs will be that much harder now because I can no longer answer their questions or offer my support. Through no fault of their own, they have lost their safety net–and that's sad.

And so it is that I have joined the ranks of the unemployed. I can live with that, for awhile. I'll spend more time with my son and work outside in the yard. They say that God doesn't close one door without opening another; except, in my case he opened a window–and so it is that I am freefalling. Will I land on my feet? You bet I will! I might suffer two broken ankles and a large measure of bruised pride, but that won't stop me. There are countless other roads to travel, and I will hold my head high as I hobble away.

Would I Lie to You?

I was amused by an article in the "This Week" section of last week's Oconto County Reporter. It was an article about Mount Sterling, a small town in Iowa, that wants to pass a new law. It seems the city council there wants to ban lying. They've got to be kidding, right? Ban lying? How would you even begin to go about passing such an ordinance, and how would you enforce it?

Still, it does make me wonder . . . Can you imagine what life would be like if everyone were totally honest? It would be almost as bad as being able to read minds. Don't get me wrong; I admire honesty as much as the next person does. I am quite familiar with its merits, and I am aware of one's moral obligation to tell the truth. However, I am also certain that little white lies came into existence to save us from ourselves.

I teach communication classes for Northeast Wisconsin Technical College. A topic we cover in one of the courses is 'self-disclosure'. This is the art of knowing how much of ourselves we should share with others. Your level of self-disclosure changes depending upon who you are with, as well as how you feel toward that person. It can also be affected by 'where' you are physically when a conversation takes place. For example, self-disclosure is easier with close friends, and within the confines of your home. People often lie as an alternative to self-disclosure because they aren't comfortable exposing their true thoughts or feelings. The textbook I use for class doesn't say that lying is a 'good' thing. In fact, it states that a lack of honesty can threaten even the strongest relationships—especially if the lies concern important issues, or if there is a pattern of continual deception. Still, talking about the merits of a "little white lie" always makes for an interesting discussion among my students. We discuss who lies, why, and what about.

We're all tempted to defend our reputations and insist that we're totally honest, but we know that isn't true. If a friend gets a terrible haircut and asks for your opinion, what do you say? *She* thinks it's the greatest—and it's way too late to glue the hair back on—so what do you tell her? Do you tell her the truth, when there's nothing to gain by doing so? Your little girl bakes cookies for the first time and insists on doing everything herself. She forgets to put in the sugar—or uses twice as much baking soda as the recipe calls for. How do they taste—are you going to be honest? Oh sure, you could say they're wonderful for a first try, but is that the truth? Or let's say a friend borrows your favorite sweater or music CD. Somehow the item gets ruined. Your friend is devastated by the loss, and finally sums up the courage to tell you. Do you add to his or her pain by honestly stating (over and over again) how much the item meant to you, or do you tell them they should forget about it because it's no big deal?

Sometimes we lie to protect ourselves, and sometimes we lie to protect the ones we love. Maybe, following a serious medical diagnosis, we tell everyone we're "fine" because to tell them the truth would be too painful . . . or maybe we promise a close friend that everything is going to be all right when we really don't have a clue. I'd hate to think that a big part of who we are depends on what we lie about, but let's be honest, it's simply impossible to always tell the truth.

Something Magic

There is magic in being a child. When you're a child, there is something unforgettable about watching the snow fall and looking for rainbows. Nothing is simple, or boring, or old. Everything is an adventure. You toss a small leaf or stick into a ditch behind your house during the spring thaw and imagine that it's a sea-going vessel, headed for some faraway land.

There is magic in the thunderstorms that frighten you in the middle of the night, and in the comfort that you found in your mother's arms. There is magic in birthdays, and holidays, and summers without school. Nothing is old, nothing is tired, and you live in wonder of what you'll be on the day you grow up, but you're just as certain that day will never come.

Later, there is something magic about being a young adult. There is a thrill in moving out and finally being on your own. Whoever forgets their first apartment, or their first kiss? Also, whoever forgets their first paycheck–that feeling that you'd just been robbed when you looked at it and wondered where the rest of the money went? There is something magical in getting a snow day off from work, buying your first car, and falling in love for the very first time. You have your own home, your own yard, and your own life. You no longer have the luxury of waiting for someone else to make your decisions for you, so you end up making your first really big mistakes. But even that's all right, because you're young and strong, and you have your whole life ahead of you to make it right.

There is something magical about growing older. There is understanding and acceptance–of both the seasons and life. Now, when the storms come, your quiet faith calms the child who still lives deep within you. You can bow out of the rat race and not even be curious about who eventually won. You are no longer at odds with the world–or yourself. You once again find yourself looking for rainbows, but now you understand the miracles that lie hidden in the colors. There's something very powerful in finally realizing that you're not in charge . . . and never were. There is magic in the moment when you can let it all go.

The Dreaded Reunion

I got the phone call the other night. Quite out of the blue a classmate–a voice from the distant past–called to inform me that our twenty-fifth class reunion would be held in July. This was no surprise. I had done the math already–way last summer, in fact. I had known it was coming, but somehow that didn't quite soften the blow.

Twenty-five years. A quarter of a century. How can 'living' cause life to go by so quickly? And how come life seems to move faster the older we get? If someone would have asked me in 1977 where I would be in twenty-five years, I would have had what I thought were all the right answers. I would have said that I'd be happily married, and definitely 'settled down'. Today, I'm not even sure what 'settled down' means. Back then, in the age of naivety and certainty, I would have painted myself as a writer with at least one book to my credit. Instead, I make my living upholstering leather seats for private jets that fly away to places I will never see. They leave trails across the sky, like the very threads of life, stretching between a beginning and an end.

Don't get me wrong, I don't mean to complain. I am happy with where my life has taken me. And, the reality is, even if I were given the chance to go back in time, there's really not much I'd do differently. Still, facing your twenty-fifth class reunion is certainly enough of a cause to make you stop and at least ponder where you've spent all that time. I've spent it raising my children, and there aren't many regrets that come with being a mom.

In four, short years, my youngest will leave for college. I've already figured it out–that's just one year shy of my *thirtieth* reunion. Maybe by then, with the last of the kids gone, I will be able to figure out what I want to be when *I* grow up. Who knows, perhaps it will be my children who become the authors; they're all pretty talented and quite creative. I'll just sit back and watch while they become famous, and happily married, and 'settled' in life. I will be sincerely happy for their success, of that I am certain.

And then, I'll just move in with them!

Changing Times

I am not old. Middle-aged, perhaps; I could live with that label. In fact, I prefer to think of myself as entering my second childhood. This theory of having a second childhood is liberating. It is a little like having grandchildren; everything is more fun the second time around.

Think about it. You're older and wiser, so it only makes sense that you'd be a lot better at being silly and spontaneous at forty than you were at the tender young age of four or five. Back then, when other kids laughed at you, you were crushed. When you're forty and people laugh, you realize one of two things. They're either laughing with you, which is a good thing–or they're laughing *at* you, which really doesn't mean anything at all. At forty, you know who you are, inside and out. Being laughed at doesn't change that.

So, having established that I am not old, I can't help but watch in awe as the world changes around me. You only have to commute to Green Bay from Oconto to know what I mean. I don't recognize much of that highway anymore. To make matters worse (or better, depending on your point of view), the four-lane highway will soon snake its way past both Lena and Oconto. And the road is not the only change. With roads, come people. In fields where corn and hay grew, year after year, there is a new kind of crop–houses. *Big* houses–the kind that people who have lived their entire lives farming that same land probably can't afford. It seems the whole county is turning into a residential subdivision; I'm just not sure where the people and the money are coming from. But I am sure that it will not end.

There are very few winding, seldom-traveled, country roads left in this area, and the people who manage to find them still insist on driving what is now their customary 60 miles an hour. Everyone is in a hurry. Why? For what? Yes, on occasion life gives us a reason to hurry–a sick child waiting at home, a pressing deadline, or maybe you have overslept. But 'rushing' has become the norm, not the exception. We schedule every hour of every day. We feel frazzled and stressed. Do you have any 'free' time? Can you remember the last time you read a good book? Do you enjoy the peace that comes from a quiet home, or have you fallen into the trap of turning on the television the very second you walk into the house, only to proceed to another room to look through the mail?

So here I am, in the prime of my second childhood, staring at the changes around me and feeling overwhelmed. Sometimes it all seems like a dream. The times are changing far too quickly. The child in me misses the simplicity that used to define country living–quiet summer evenings, no traffic on the road, nothing that needed to be done, no place else you had to be. It's harder missing something at my age, because you know it's never coming back.

At times I choose to believe it's all a dream, but then I hear a shrill, ringing sound. It's someone's cell phone. I must be awake after all, for I'm being forced to listen to half of a conversation I have no right to hear. I feel guilty, like I'm eavesdropping (and I've been raised in another age, so I know that is rude), but the person with the phone is oblivious to my discomfort. The world revolves for only them. I'd like to snatch the phone away, or tell the person to take their conversation someplace private, but I don't. Heck, being in my second childhood, a part of me is very tempted to simply kick them in the shin and run away. Thankfully, the adult in me has more self-control. Besides, who am I kidding? I can't run that fast anymore.

Across the Miles

I lost my very best friend today. Well, I suppose 'lost' is not the most appropriate word to use. I know exactly where she is; she moved to Baraboo. The thing is, she's not going to be 'here' anymore, and that hurts more than I care to say.

I've only known Bonnie for five years. I'll admit that five years is not a long time to know someone, especially when you consider that there are veteran friendships which last for half a century or more. Perhaps you know of such a long-standing friendship, or perhaps you are blessed enough to be such a friend. But the value and strength of a relationship is not measured in years; nor, I suppose, is it measured in how close the people are geographically located to one another. The distinguishing characteristic of strong, binding relationships is simply that they last. But entering into and maintaining such relationships are not two of my strong points. With the exception of family, people in my life tend to come and go—like whispers in the night, or warm breezes that pause to stir my soul, then quietly move on. They flair, then fade, and eventually become only memories that I keep with me long after life has carried them on.

And so it will be with Bonnie. Though I am deeply pained by her leaving, in my heart I am happy for her. She is moving to be closer to her children and grandchildren, who are the center of her life. But there is always the flip side to that proverbial coin. In this case, the flip side is my loss. For five years, eight to ten hours a day, five or six days a week, we have worked side by side and grown accustomed to the quirks that make each of us unique. True friendship is a real and tangible thing, and we shared all the symptoms. With only a glance, we knew what the other was thinking. Without being told, we knew what the other would say. We talked about men, and life, and each other. We gossiped and laughed, sighed and vented. If I was cranky or joyous, she was there just the same. That's how it is with true friends. You are who you are; there's no pretending.

But now, there will be miles between us. I'm not much good at writing letters, funny as that may seem. I brandish the same old excuse that I've used time and again—there's just no time and simply not enough hours in the day. . If I were honest, though, I would admit that letters are all about details—a recalling of the fine points that go on in one's life. When people move away and move on with their lives, the details of what 'once was' matter less and less. By next month, I doubt Bonnie will care too very much about how many orders our department filled, or how many hours we had to work. And I'm going to be absolutely terrible at sharing her joy over a grandchild's first steps, especially after a fifty-five hour workweek. It's a lot like being on separate roads that are heading in opposite directions . . . you keep hollering back and forth, comforted by the fact that you can still hear the familiar voice. But, in time, the voice grows fainter, and the calls are fewer and further between. Life carries us all onward; no one stands still.

That's not to say that friendships, and their blessings, are temporary things that are doomed to ultimately fail. A true friendship, like true love, seeks out what is best in the other person, and what is best for itself as well. We struggle, and grow, and change–and through it all, friends move in and out of our lives, like angels in disguise. We think of them, sometimes years after they have gone, and we smile. We are better for knowing them. We are stronger, and gentler, and more compassionate. Perhaps it is because they meant so much to us that we try to be a little more like they are–and thus we grow. The power of such a friendship is immeasurable. And whether that friend is just around the block or somewhere further away–like Baraboo–they will always be just as close as our heart.

The Easy Way

Just my luck. After I have spent nearly two years counting calories and fat grams, *now* the offer comes in the mail. It seems Prevention Magazine has a new weight-loss program, and they're holding a 'test pilot' spot just for me! It's called 'Banish Your Belly, Butt & Thighs Forever.' Their program not only claims to deliver fast results, it requires 'no hard exercise, no giving up my favorite foods, and no carrot sticks' (unless I want them). And the best part is that I can try it free for 21 days! After that, if I like the results, I can pay for the program by making four easy installments of just $7.49 each. It sounds so simple, it's actually tempting. The easy way always is.

As it so happened, I received the Harriet Carter catalog on the same day. Should I decide that 'Banish Your Belly, Butt and Thighs Forever' isn't for me, this catalog has plenty of other options I can choose from. The AbSlide on the back cover claims it will give me 'a firm stomach, chest, shoulders, and arms in just three minutes a day!'–and it's mine for $39.98, plus $7.98 postage and handling. (Did you ever wonder why these places charge you for both postage *and* handling? Wouldn't you think that you'd have to handle something in order to send it, so the charge for one should really include both?) A cheaper version on page 70, the Exercise Wheel, makes basically the same claims–but also provides benefits for your calf muscles. It's only $6.98, plus $3.98 postage and (you guessed it) handling.

No time to exercise? The Super Slim Briefs on page 66 reduce extra pounds *and* cellulite by using heat and massage to 'break down fatty tissues'. The bonus part is they make you look thinner just by putting them on! They were $17.98, but now they can be yours for only $12.95, plus $4.98 for you know what. On page 65 there's a Step-Away Exerciser; on page 60, a 'Lose Weight with Apple Vinegar Book'; on page 50, A Pedal Exerciser; on page 44, an 'Invisible Tummy Trimmer'. And here's something else the catalog offers, if you go too far and lose too much, the 'Bigger Bust' tablets on page 43 will add inches back on that crucial area in as little as two months.

If only it were that simple. I suppose if products like these worked, we'd all be in shape. But anyone who's lost weight or tried to get in shape knows it takes time, and hard work, and commitment. The important things in life, the ones that really matter, are never easy. Getting in shape is tough; so is believing in yourself and where your life is going. Finding love, commitment and an existence that reflects your beliefs are all tough chores. That's what makes them worthwhile;

that's what makes them important.

If you should decide to lose weight, it won't be a product you find in a catalog that makes it happen. Whether you succeed or fail depends on how hard you believe. We can all be as successful, or thin, or happy, as we want. We just have to believe. Along with that belief, we also have to be willing and able to work for it, sometimes very hard. That's just how life works; there's no easy way.

So, I guess Prevention Magazine will have to give my 'test pilot' spot to someone else. I'll continue my membership at the Bond Center and spend a few more hours on the walking track and in the weight room. Yes, there are times when it's inconvenient and I really don't feel like going, but it's something I do for me, and something that I believe in. Also, by doing that, I can leave the postage and handling charge for someone else to pay.

Who's Calling, Please?

The telephone is an amazing thing. That we can dial a friend's number and, seconds later, hear their phone ringing at the other end of the continent–or on the other side of the world–is no small feat. Ever since I was a child, I have always been in awe of the speed with which we are connected, or disconnected, all through the simple workings of a phone.

When I was growing up, the telephone was mysterious and black. It hung by the refrigerator and was mostly silent. It was something my parents used when they had business to tend to, or a family member to check up on. Yes, you could also talk to the neighbors on it, sometimes without even dialing first. You'd just pick up the receiver and there they'd be, chatting away with someone, anyone, in the whole wide world. Sometimes they talked forever, or sometimes they'd pick up when you were talking and the ominous, repetitive 'clicking' sound warned you it was time to hang up and let someone else use the line. Incoming calls also had to be shared. For us, two quick rings meant we could answer it; one long ring told us the call was for the family down the road.

Despite what children are told, sharing was not always a good thing–at least not when it came to phone lines. As likely as not, when one party chose to tie up the line, tempers would flare. This was especially true in farming communities during the haying season. Somehow, haying season had a way of producing short tempers all the way around. But, if one party needed to call the local implement dealer to check on a part, and the other party was leisurely sharing her grandma's secret recipe for pumpkin pie and zucchini bread–with all the variations–you knew that words were about to be exchanged. Throw a stray rain cloud into that picture, and you had some real excitement!

Times sure have changed. Now we all have private telephone lines, with access to all the options that go with them. We have caller I.D., call waiting, call forwarding, call blocking, last number redial, *69, *70, *71, *89 and whatever other options you might want to throw into the mix. If someone wants to talk to us in this enlightened age, they have several options; we can be called, beeped, paged or buzzed. And the creativity doesn't stop there. If we aren't available to answer a call, there are trusty answering machines ready and waiting. Better yet, your computer can answer the call (if you have the right program). Or, for another small monthly fee, the phone company (or any of a number of other communication specialists) will do it as well.

I try to keep it simple. I just settle for a caller I.D. Upon returning home, I check the display unit, note who called, and return the calls I feel are important. There are days I am truly glad I was at work–such as when 'Unavailable' shows up on my display unit fourteen times at twelve-minute intervals. Those who own caller I.D.s quickly learn that 'Unavailable' means *salesman*, and the call is best left unanswered. While I was at work and slaving away, the poor phone was also busy and ringing off the hook, but there was nobody there to pick it up.

This 'new age' has brought many options and choices that allow us to customize how we communicate with one another. We can use our phone lines for paging, for faxing, or even for 'surfing the net'. Heck, we can spend our entire paycheck (and then some) right over the phone line–without ever leaving the house! And the magic doesn't stop where the phone line ends. 'Cordless' and 'cellular' have come to our rescue, so now we can be reached no matter where we are–in the garden, in our car, fishing, jogging–absolutely anywhere. Your cellular phones can even connect you to the Internet, and the entire world beyond, from wherever you desire. It's hard to believe how far we've come. Really.

As with most people who wake up one morning and suddenly realize they have a past spreading out behind them, I kind of miss the 'old' days–you know, when telephones were used to really 'communicate' with each other. The telephone line wasn't a salesman's lifeline, or a stalker's method of finding his next victim. When the phone rang, you actually answered it with a sense of wonder, curious about who was on the other end and what it was they wanted to share. Phones brought people closer and kept us all in touch. Period. They didn't ring incessantly, at all hours. They didn't slip pushy salespeople (or politicians) into our homes when supper was finally being served. They didn't threaten, bore, or annoy. They weren't space-age tools struggling to hold the world together. They were just a luxury that allowed two friends to stay in touch. And, if your friend also happened to be on your party line, staying in touch was often as simple as lifting the receiver and holding it to your ear.

On Being a Man

After forty-three years of living, I've learned a handful of things. One thing I've learned is that I'm glad I'm not a man. For starters, I like being me. I like the 'flexibility' of being a woman. We can be strict, or soft, or quiet, or bold, and nobody really thinks twice about it. In fact, we can be absolutely impossible and the world will write it off as 'it's that time of month.' It's no secret that we can get away with a lot and blame it on PMS. Men, sadly, don't have that option.

That's not to say that men can't get moody. After all, moodiness is a 'human' condition, not a gender-induced state. But my experience is that men don't suffer from it quite as much. To a point, they are who they are, regardless of what time of month it might be. That doesn't change at the blink of an eye or the drop of a hat. You can take them or leave them (just don't try to change them!) They're good or bad, shallow or intense, sincere or two-faced, just like women can be, but women are much better at keeping such traits hidden away. In fact, when I meet new people, I can honestly say that it takes me a lot longer to figure out what 'makes a woman tick' or what really lies buried inside her head, than it does for me to figure out a new man. I find that fact disturbing, if for no other reason than I am a woman. And, if *I* have such a hard time figuring women out, I don't envy any man who's trying to do the same thing.

I'm not saying that women are naturally deceptive. I think 'cautious' may be a better word for it. Maybe we're still evolving; I mean, just look at the last century and the changes it's held. As the saying goes, women have come a long way, but at what price? We want to be everything to everyone, and we want to have it all. We want to be free to be able to raise kids, hold down a job, maintain a household, be a good mate, interact in the community, and have enough time left over to help reshape the world. We want to be bold, and strong, and smart, and independent–but we still want to be loved, and cherished, and even protected at times. I suppose the real trick lies in determining what we want at any one specific moment. Are we looking for success or serenity, advancement or stability? If *we're* not sure, how could any man have a clue?

I'm not saying that all of these changes are bad; I'm just saying that they're confusing. There's no doubt that we're finally headed in the right direction. The road to fulfillment now stretches out ahead of all of us–and woe to any man (or woman) who gets in our way! The only problem is that we're not exactly sure where the road leads. We've got a pretty good handle on what lies behind us, but no one can say for sure what lies ahead.

So, what is a man to make of all of this? I can't say. How much easier it must have been to keep it all straight back in the 'good old days'–back when men went to work and women stayed home to tend to the house and kids. In a great many ways, those were simpler times. Back then, women weren't afraid to accept help when it was offered, because we understood that men wanted to give it; we weren't threatened by being called the 'weaker sex', because we knew it wasn't true; we never had to change our own oil, or pay someone else to do it. Let's face it, the line that divided what men and women did–and who they were–was a lot clearer back then. Today, there's only a shadow where it once existed.

I'm not sure what it takes to make today's woman happy, and I'm not alone. There might be a handful of men out there who have managed to figure it out, but from what I've seen it's all too confusing. If a man offers too much help, we complain about being smothered; if they don't offer any, we label them as self-centered and thoughtless. If they pay more than their fair share during an evening out on the town, they're threatening our sense of independence; if they don't, they're cheap. Once upon a time, men could 'fix' our problems and women weren't threatened by that fact. Today, we pretend the problems don't exist–and no man better suggest they do.

So, to be very honest, I'm glad I'm not a man. It's confusing enough just being me. Whether it's a good thing or a bad thing, women have rewritten a lot of the basic rules and expected men to keep up. A few men have managed to do just that, but it seems that a great deal more were lost somewhere far behind. A lot has changed between the genders in the last century, and it has little to do with who brings home the bacon and who fries it up. It seems that, in our attempt to level the playing field, we've changed so many of the rules that no one seems to know how to play the game anymore, let alone be able to know the score.

Promises

I've made a lot of promises in my life. They've come in all shapes and sizes. Some are legal and binding, like I promised the bank I'd make my house payments, and I promised the Ford Motor Company I'd pay for my car. Even my smaller, monthly bills are promises of a sort; I am allowed unlimited use of electricity, heating fuel and a telephone with the understanding that I will pay for what I use. These are obligations I live with on a daily basis.

It's an unspoken promise that I owe my employer an honest day's work for an honest day's pay. I owe my pets a safe home, some compassion, and a bit of my time. I promised my kids my support and my love. I offer my friends a silent promise of an ear they can bend and a helping hand in their time of need. I owe it to my parents to lead an honest and fulfilling life. I promise my God all my gratitude for this world He has made, and my chance to live in it. I have made a great many promises. Some are easier to keep than others. And, being human, I guess I haven't kept them all, but I try.

Where I most often fall short is in keeping the promises I make to myself. When there are not enough hours in the day, I forsake my free time and instead try to accomplish some other task. I help my son with homework instead of working on my novel; I fold the laundry in place of reading a chapter in a good book; I clean out the refrigerator instead of taking a walk through my garden. It seems I truly value the promises I make, unless I'm promising something to myself. Maybe that's why it's taken me over twenty years to get to chapter thirty-six in the novel I'm writing; too many other things had to come first.

If you're anything like me, we've got to start keeping our promises–*especially* the ones we make to ourselves. Think about it; when someone lies to us on a regular basis, we tend to stop listening to them. We lose our trust in them, and no longer value what they have to say. The same is true when we lie to ourselves. It can be argued that there is way too much "I", "me" and "mine" in the world today, but there is also a lot of self-denial. There *is* more to life than bringing home a paycheck, or a parent. Yes, those things are important, but so are you. You can't be a great employee, or the world's greatest parent, if you're not being good to yourself. With that in mind, be kind to yourself. Be compassionate. If you bribe yourself with the promise of a treat when you get the job done, you'd better deliver the goods. No one else will be able to trust you if you lie to yourself.

One Bad Apple

Have you ever wondered what the world would be like if everyone was honest? I never gave it much thought, but that question popped into my head the other day. It was one of those moments when I was busy doing something that didn't require much thought, so of course one popped in. The longer I actually thought about it, the more I realized that the world would be a very different place if we could all just trust each other.

For starters, there would be no locks on our doors, or on our cars. We would not have to 'secure' our belongings, or pay an insurance premium to protect them against theft or vandalism. We would have no keys to lose, and no combinations to memorize, because nothing would be locked. Our cars would start at the push of a button and anyone could do it; even so, the car would always be right where we'd left it.

Banks wouldn't offer safety deposit boxes, and we could leave our 'extra' money in the cookie jar, where it would be safe and sound. Maybe credit cards wouldn't even exist, because we could all buy something just on the power of our word. In such a world, if we promised to make a payment on the 10th of each month, our creditor would know the money would be there–and in cold, hard cash–simply because we were honest.

I wonder what the prices at stores would be like if everyone was honest. How much would our jeans or new shoes cost if we weren't all paying for the security systems and the lost revenue businesses suffer at the hands of thieves? Have you ever walked through the scanner at the exit of a department store and had the alarm go off? Did you feel about two inches high, even though you knew every item in your bag was paid for? Those scanners are there because dishonesty exists; but, for those of us who pay for the items in our bags, the alarm is irritating enough to make us want to sue the store for defamation of character!

This brings us to the court systems. If everyone was honest, we wouldn't need so many judges and lawyers. There would be far fewer trials than we have today, and no one would have to be 'sworn in' at the beginning of his or her testimony because we would tell the truth, just as a matter of character. Think about it–we'd exist in a world where no one would be defaulted, cheated, or 'ripped off.'

And then we have to consider the changes honesty would bring to the family. Parents would always know that their teenagers were telling the truth when asked where they were at 1 a.m. Mothers would no longer wonder how the vase in the bedroom got broken, where the missing pizza went, or who ate the last cookie. Also, there would be no secrets between husbands and wives. Now there's a scary thought! Meals and waistlines would be commented on honestly. Maybe the court systems wouldn't be so quiet after all–at least not for the divorce lawyers.

Still, all in all, the world would be a much better place. There would be less stress and worry, and a whole lot less gossip. Oh yes, one last thought. Please note that I haven't even brushed on the topic of politics. It is an election year yet again, and we'll soon have a new president coming onboard. It might be best to just steer clear of that entire arena! Even *I'm* not creative enough to ponder honesty in a political setting. I tried to get a more professional opinion on the topic, but George Bush, Sr., wouldn't offer his view on the matter. I guess there's more than a little truth in the saying that one bad apple can spoil it for the whole bunch.

Inspiration

Everywhere we look today, it seems books, magazines, and a variety of experts are selling us the secrets to true inspiration. The "Chicken Soup" book series has mushroomed to a point where there is a version of the book for practically everyone. There is *Chicken Soup for the Pet Lover's Soul, Chicken Soup for the Writers' Soul, Chicken Soup for the Teenage Soul*, and on and on. And it doesn't end there. Almost every magazine on the newsstand has at least one article geared toward helping you find true happiness. In one issue of Good Housekeeping, the cover boasted *The Happiness Report! Surprising News on How to Make Your Spirit Soar*. Of course, the article below it stated *I Lost 20 lbs! How 10 Moms Took It Off*. If I could lose twenty pounds, I know my spirits would soar! Another article, *Make More $$$ . . . A Sexy New Savings Bond*, rounded off what the magazine had to offer. Perhaps I'm way out of touch, but I fail to see how a savings bond can be sexy. Still, all of the articles had one thing in common—they tempted you with possible happiness. *If I only knew the secret, or lost some weight, or found a better way to handle my money, I'd be happy. If only . . .*

May I be so bold as to ask, if it's that easy to be inspired, why aren't we? With so many experts showing us the way, with so many good books already published on the topic (and more coming every day), why do so many of us feel we are lost? Children are abused, neglected, misguided. Marriages are empty and very apt to fail. Jobs are unfulfilling. Let's face it; life is simply not what we thought it would be. The 'answers' (according to the experts) are everywhere, but we just can't seem to grasp them. For those to whom this article does not apply—those few, contented beings who have managed to 'find' themselves in this chaotic world—here is your chance to sit back and smile. You already know the secret. For the rest of us, though, here goes . . .

I believe, quite simply, that we are elephants. We are strong and intelligent creatures, but we've been conditioned to live as we are living. Have you ever been to a circus and wondered how such massive animals can be tied with nothing more than a length of rope? You and I both know the elephant could very easily break that rope and find freedom, at least for a while. You and I know that; the problem is, the elephant doesn't. He knew it once, but he's forgotten. You see, when the elephant was very young, it was tied with a sturdy logging chain. Despite its best efforts and hours of struggling, it could not break free. Over time, it finally accepted the fact that it could not escape. It learned that, when its leg was held fast, it was foolish to fight. Thus, adult elephants are held fast by mere ropes simply because they *believe* they are.

For people, there is an opposite truth. Finding happiness involves *believing* that we can. Many times, *we* are the biggest roadblocks stopping us from having whatever we desire. We don't think we can do it; we don't think we deserve it; we believe we will fail because we've failed in the past. We are like the elephant, trapped by false beliefs; yet, in reality, the whole world is ours for the taking! I have a sign on my desk that reads, "I can only be what I give myself permission to be." It's a saying given to us by the Cherokee and I read it daily. It's easy to *read* those words; actually following through and granting myself the permission is a little harder to do.

Do you really want to find inspiration? Then simply believe; *allow* yourself to dream; *allow* yourself to achieve. Grant yourself the simple permission to be something. Shake off that 'elephantarian' frame of mind and pull free! If you're searching for inspiration, you are not alone. There are roadmaps to it everywhere you look; but, to really find it, the best place to begin looking is inside yourself.

Have You Ever Wondered?

The summer is officially over. Seeing that the familiar, yellow buses are once again collecting our children on a daily basis and transporting them to and from school, I thought some of you adults might want to exercise your brains as well. The following is a list of things I've been wondering about. If you can enlighten me on any one of them, please do! You can reach me via e-mail at kcberg1@centurytel.net. Here goes:

#1: How come every time a product says "new and improved", it isn't?

#2: How come printing a statement on a box that reads "some settling of contents may occur during shipping and handling" makes it legal for them to sell us half a box of cereal?

#3: How come, whenever the price of milk is at an all-time low, consumers still pay the same price for butter, milk, cream and cheese? Where's all that extra money going?

#4: How come grain farmers only get a few cents for their contribution to a box of cereal?

#5: How come we can send people to the moon and back, and we still can't come up with a better invention to close a loaf of bread than a twist-tie?

#6: When you put a thought out of your head, where does it go?

#7: Why do all new shoes suddenly have the same length shoelaces–which are usually ten inches too long?

#8: How come "free offers" usually aren't, and "free checking" usually isn't?

#9: During a sale, how can an item possibly be "as low as $75.99 or lower"? Doesn't "as low as" mean that's the absolute bottom price?

#10: How come every sale a store has is "the best sale of the year" or "the best in their history", but the prices don't really seem to show it?

#11: How come Christmas cards (and sales!) come earlier every year?

#12: How come when someone says, "It's the least I can do," it usually is?

#13: Do we really get wiser as we get older, or are we just too tired to argue?

#14: How come "easy open cans" aren't and "stay tight lids" don't?

#15: When the snow melts, where does all the 'white' go?

#16: How come every time my computer asks me, "Are you sure you want to delete this file?" I chicken out and hit cancel?

Rise and Shine

Let's suppose that you are lucky enough to have a job. And let's further suppose that you work the first shift. It's 4:30 a.m. and the alarm goes off. As you reach over to silence it, what words run through your mind? I worked the first shift for many years, and I can tell you what words ran through *my* mind everyday when the alarm clock woke me. Actually, I can't tell you, because I don't like to use that kind of language when I write. Suffice to say the first words that came to my mind at that time of day weren't very lady-like! Add to this scenario the fact that I kept my alarm clock on the other side of the room, which forced me to get out of bed and actually walk over to shut it off. Believe me when I say that I had plenty of time to think all sorts of words on that morning trek to the clock. A few minutes later, I was in the shower and telling myself–over and over, day after day–that there had to be a better way to make a living, if only I knew what it was.

If this all sounds familiar, maybe you have the same problem I was suffering from. Sure, I could simply say that I was never a morning person, but that's not what my frustration was all about. Not really. In actuality, I was suffering from a lack of passion, perhaps even a mid-life crisis. I was tired of spending my time doing things that had no meaning. I felt that there simply had to be more to life than earning a paycheck. Sure, that paycheck allowed me to make my house payment, which gave me a place to sleep (until that damn alarm clock went off again!), but I felt certain that there had to be more. I wanted to do something that mattered. I wanted to make a difference in the world, and the lives of those around me. And once–just once–I wanted to get up in the morning and be thrilled at the work that awaited me that day.

Perhaps those are some of the reasons why I took up writing. It helped to vent my frustration. It was a passion that filled a void; it allowed me to reach out to others and added meaning to my life. Still, it's not what I do after the alarm clock rings. It doesn't pay the bills, or feed the hungry wolves. It's how I choose to live, but it's not how I make my living.

I had (and still have) options; we all do. We can find another job, or go back to school to obtain a degree. Once we get miserable enough, we find a way to change. But, until that day comes, there will always be that alarm clock to answer to. To make matters worse, for those of us who live where there's a thing called Daylight Savings

Time, it rings an hour earlier for about half of the year. That's definitely not a pleasant thought!

So think about it when the alarm clock is ringing tomorrow morning. If you're rolling over with a smile and hitting the snooze button contentedly, then count your blessings as you step into the shower and begin your day. Be grateful for the simple blessing of contentment. But, if the alarm clock annoys you, and life seems to be pushing you (kicking and screaming) toward scary options and strange, new horizons, then I wish you a safe journey. But even more, I wish you passion. Seize the moment! Dare to do it! Grab each day that life has to offer and spend it doing what really matters. After all, each new day is really much more than simply another chance to rise and shine.

Old Souls

Having been given the ability to speculate and reason, people tend to spend a great deal of time thinking about life and death. We question what happens around us, and to us. We use terms like "destiny", "fate", and "luck" to explain why some people's lives are so much better (or worse) than our own. We analyze choices and make plans, all in an effort to gain some control over this thing that we call life. Then, when we are tired of thinking about life, we wonder what's on the 'other side'. We question the existence of heaven and hell. Is life followed by punishment, or reward, based on how we've lived our lives, or is there simply a large void waiting to claim us?

I was raised Catholic, and I do believe in an existence beyond this life. I believe that we have souls, or spirits, and that we continue to 'exist' long after the flesh has failed. I also believe that having a soul makes us accountable for our actions and choices. So, in essence, our free will gives us the option of choosing our own paths, and we subsequently choose to be good, bad, or somewhere in-between. This, to me, is all pretty "cut and dried".

But I hold another belief as well which is not part of my Catholic upbringing. I believe in "old souls". Some might call it reincarnation, but it goes a little further than that. It is a theory that, for me anyway, explains so many things about life, and fate, and relationships. I don't remember where I first encountered the idea; most likely it was in some book I'd stumbled upon. And although the source of the theory escapes me, I do remember the theory itself.

Like reincarnation, it is the belief that we live over and over again. We do this until we've learned everything we need to know, or until we are ready for heaven or whatever else may await us. This pattern is similar to reincarnation, but it also goes one step further; it embraces the belief that some souls always travel together, guiding one another and learning from one another. In each successive life, the identities change. For example, in one life, you may be best friends; in another, parent and child; in yet another, husband and wife. Beyond your physical existence, there is a spiritual bond that holds you together through time and space. You share each life's journey, but with no recollection of doing so.

You're scowling and shaking your head; you're certain I've finally 'lost it'; but think about it. It explains why some people seem so familiar, even though you've never met. It explains the easy manner with which we merge our lives with some people–the impression that we've shared time and space before, the fleeting sense of déjà vu. Viewed in the light of this theory, 'love at first sight' is not a mystery, but a union on a spiritual level that the heart embraces even while the mind struggles to understand. It is why, spending time with some people, feels like 'coming home', no matter where we are at the time.

My son is an old soul. Call me crazy, if you will, but he didn't cry when he was born. When they wrapped him in a blanket and placed him in my arms, he looked around with wisdom in his big, blue eyes that I cannot explain. A thought came to me, 'Yes, he's been here before.' This is the same child who, as a two year-old child, clutched story books and begged to be read to; and who now, as an ancient teenager, is telling me that he has no intentions of dating anytime soon. His reasoning? He says he has to figure out who *he* is before he can figure out anyone else. His soul is aged far beyond his years.

Old souls exist; I am certain of it. Think about this theory the next time you lock eyes with a stranger, and wonder when you've seen those eyes before. Think about it when you instinctively know that you should trust (or distrust) someone you've just met, or when you find yourself falling in love at first sight. The belief in old souls is not a denial of heaven and hell, or anything in-between. It is not a lack of faith, but an affirmation of it. God was quoted as having said that we would never walk alone. However, He never said He'd be the only one walking with us.

Resisting Change

Old age has a way of sneaking up on you. One day, you look in the mirror and you find that dreaded first gray hair. Because it's not content to live alone, it soon invites many friends to join it. Go ahead; pluck them out as fast as you find them–it won't do any good. The gray hairs will keep coming. At some point, your vision begins to fail. Things just aren't as clear as they used to be; you squint to focus and move the object closer or farther away in an effort to see it. Before you know it, your feet and legs tire more quickly, and it seems to take longer to get moving in the morning. All of these symptoms are signs that the years are slipping past.

Last week, old age nailed me right between the eyes–and not in the manner I had been expecting. I teach an assortment of written communication classes for the local technical colleges. True to the teaching profession, I was correcting some essays my students had submitted. As I went through the papers, I was busy using red ink to mark where students had failed to place two spaces after every period. That is the rule, isn't it? You place one space after commas, colons, and semi-colons, and two spaces after periods, exclamation points, and question marks. In other words, you type two spaces to mark the end of each sentence. Or so I thought.

As I came across more and more papers with a single space after the periods, I became suspicious that perhaps the world of writing had changed overnight and I hadn't been informed. To satisfy my curiosity, I checked online for more current rules on punctuation. To my surprise and dismay, I soon learned that they don't teach that anymore. In fact, I discovered that typing two spaces after a period is considered to be an "archaic" form of writing.

There you have it. In an instant, I was placed in the archaic category (no doubt the same category that contains words like "thou" and "thee"). I couldn't believe it! The explanation offered for this change was that modern word processors and computer word-processing programs often right-justify written material. Using two spaces at the end of each sentence causes wide, annoying gaps in the text. Who'd have known? I phoned my parents, my grown daughters, and several people whom I work with. I asked them all, point blank, without any explanation, "How many spaces do you type after a period?" To my relief, they had all been taught the same as me. We fear loneliness in this archaic realm.

So there you have it. Old age (or the archaic period) has arrived in my life. In my own defense (and despite suddenly facing extinction, as all archaic things must), I have refused to color my hair, I have ignored my sore feet and legs, and I am still forcing myself to roll out of bed at 4 a.m. without too much complaining about my aches and pains–but I refuse to put only one space after a period. It just doesn't feel right. I yearn for and am comfortable with that little extra space between one thought and another. You see, I can only be forced to conform to a certain degree–after all, you know what they say about trying to teach an old dog new tricks.

The Echo of Footsteps

It is September 18th, but no hurried and excited footsteps echo through the halls of the small Catholic grade school in Lena, WI this year. No students weave in and out of the classrooms, headed for the gym, or the one-room library, or the lunchroom, or the playground. The familiar sound of the recess or dismissal bell no longer fills the hall, followed by the noisy clamor of happy children, heading out for play or home. The teachers and students are all gone, having left the building on the last day of school in the spring for the final time. The only thing that remains is the smell of lunch being prepared by caring hands–but it is being catered to the public school across the road, whose cafeteria is under renovation.

Yes, we are all told that change is unavoidable. The small school had struggled financially for years, holding on by a thread and more than one prayer. I have no doubt that the students who would have attended this school in the years to come will be taught well in the public school across the road. They will learn to read and write in larger classrooms with more modern books and equipment. They will make friends, discover new realities, and eventually grow up. But as their learning begins, what has ended?

To permanently close the doors on a school is to close the door on a million memories and another million possibilities of what might have been. In reality, the small school was nothing more than an outdated facility that had served its purpose and outlived the role it had been built for. There was a time when education and religion walked hand in hand; it was the backbone of the small, rural communities across our great country. In some places, that union has survived, but those places are getting fewer and much farther in-between. It seems as if, in our struggle to accomplish a separation of church and state, religion and faith have been hidden away–as though to practice them is shameful. It would seem that God no longer has a place in our day-to-day lives.

I find this all very sad and confusing. What are we if not spiritual beings? Why should those who lack faith dictate when and where we can practice ours? I know these aren't the specific reasons why the Catholic grade school in Lena closed, but everything in life is connected. Some of my fondest memories and greatest friendships were formed in that school. I raced through those halls and studied in those small classrooms. Every other year, I got to move to a new room, as two grades were taught by one teacher in each separate room.

84

I ate in that cafeteria; played on that playground; and attended Phy. Ed. class, and basketball games, and Christmas pageants in the gym. So did all three of my children. That was a good thing.

It is a matter of record that a large percentage of some of the brightest students to ever graduate Lena High School attended that small, Catholic grade school. Good things happened in that school. Quality education took place, bonds were formed, and memories were made. Now the school is closed. An era has ended. But like tiny ripples in a pond, the impact that small school had on its students will spiral outward, touching more and more lives as it grows.

Ultimately, school doors are not so hard to lock–maybe even forever–but faith and hope cannot be so easily contained. What that small school stood for, and the hope that it gave the children over so many years, will continue to live and grow. The past students carry it forth in their lives, like a shield against an ever-darkening world. That shield and our faith are constant companions as we move through our lives. They are the soft footsteps of unseen companions traveling by our side; they are an echo that stretches down now-empty corridors, and behind the locked doors. We are stronger, and better, for having them, for they save us from walking alone.

I've Been Thinking . . .

It has occurred to me that I think too much. All of my children suffer from the same affliction. That is not to say that we're more intelligent than most; 'thinking', by itself, should not be confused with intelligence. In fact, I am quite certain that there's no connection between how *much* we think and whether we're right or wrong. It simply means that our brains always seem to be in overdrive mode. Thinking can be a lot like eating or talking–more is not necessarily a good thing, and practice alone does not guarantee we ever get better at it.

Let me give you an example of what I mean by this. I recently had to change the antennae wire for my TV. This particular chore involved dragging the ladder out of the garage and climbing up on the roof. It also required that I pull the old wire out of the small hole drilled through my foundation so I could feed the new wire through in its place. These two tasks were not, by themselves, overly difficult to do. In preparation for the chore, I bought the necessary equipment (a new cable and connectors), and promptly began to 'think' the job through.

First, I formed a mental checklist of all the tools I would need while perched on the roof. The list included pliers, a razor blade, and electrical tape. I certainly didn't want to crawl all the way up on the roof and have to make an unnecessary trip back down. I would also have to deal with the bee nests on the south side of the house (which were located between me and the roof) and the spiders in the basement (which guard the hole where the antenna wire runs through). By thinking the job through, I felt more prepared to tackle the chore. After all, I'm about as clumsy as the proverbial ox–wearing a blindfold–so I didn't want to go up and down a ladder (or stay perched on the roof) any more than I absolutely had to.

Now, thinking a job through involves picturing yourself actually tackling the job, from beginning to end. I began by envisioning myself crawling up the ladder and onto the roof. This is where I mentally encountered my first problem. What would happen if I accidentally knocked the ladder over once I was up there? I'd be trapped. How would I ever get down? How long would it be before someone came to my rescue? When I'd begun envisioning this job, I'd recently fed my son, so I knew that it would be hours before he'd get hungry and decide to leave his room to come looking for me. In fact, it would have probably been well after dark. Besides, he'd never think of looking on the roof anyway! I could tell him I was going up there, just for my own peace of mind, but it wouldn't do much good. If my comments to him don't involve food or video games, he doesn't seem to really hear. So, if I did knock the ladder down, waiting to be rescued by my son did not seem like a very good choice.

That meant that I would have to have a plan 'B'. This was before I owned a cordless phone, and cell phones hadn't made it into my universe, so that meant that plan 'B' involved jumping. I try to envision that. Which side of the house was closest to the ground, and would therefore be the wisest side to jump from? Now that may sound like a stupid question, but my house sits on a hill and the distance from eave to ground varies greatly from one side to the next. Still trying to avoid the 'jumping' scenario, I imagine trying to climb onto my maple tree. Several of its smaller branches are brushing against the side of the house. But it's just a little tree; only nine years old. I'd probably break it off or fall out of it. That didn't sound like a very good plan, so I was back to jumping.

It soon became obvious that the side of the house by the fallen ladder would be my best bet, simply because it overlooks a deck. As opposed to actually 'jumping', I envisioned myself sliding off the edge of the roof–very slowly–gripping the black, asphalt shingles with my fingers until the very last second (I'd better add a pair of gloves to the list), then dropping the few feet to the deck. I'd have to be careful not to swing my feet, or I might break one of the windows that look out onto the deck. However, as I envisioned this controlled slide, I realized that I'd probably pull off the rain gutter using this approach–which would give me another job to add to my "to do" list. I'd be pondering the steps to that task for a month! No, it would probably be best to simply jump–or wait for the maple tree to grow a little.

Anyway, I think you get the idea. This is what a simple job becomes when you think too much–you're exhausted before you even begin! And my children are the same way–especially my one daughter. Sometimes she calls to discuss some project she's been thinking about. In a nutshell, she'll say, "If I do this, then *this* could happen, but if I do *that* then it won't be as good. But I can't just not do anything! I know–I'll do this *before* that, then the other thing will go just fine! Unless . . ." Sometimes she discusses the project in such detail that *I'm* the one who gets tired!

The bottom line is, I eventually took the bull by the horns, gathered my tools, and got the job done. I killed the bees, swept away the spiders, had all the right tools, and made sure I didn't fall off the ladder. The rain gutter is still attached to the eave, the antenna is positioned, the new wire is in place and my TV works great now. I guess there's a lot to be said for good planning. Good planning ensures that the job goes well. Hmm. It sounds like there's an article in there somewhere. I'll have to give it some more thought.

Back It Up? You've Got To Be Kidding!

I was raised on a dairy farm, and it was a wonderful life. It was also a very busy life, and there was never a shortage of chores to do. I had four siblings, and we all pitched in when it came to getting the chores done. With the exception of my older sister, who tended to spend her time doing house work and wouldn't have gotten caught dead in the barn, all of the children helped out with the farm work in one aspect or another.

My two brothers are both older than I am. Still, despite their 'maturity' and brawn, if memory serves me correctly, they were a lot better at handling the 'machinery' and 'fieldwork' part of farming than they were at dealing with the 'animal' side. I recall that they just didn't have the patience necessary to work with cows. They somehow believed that cows should do what they are told, when they are told, and that they should do it without hesitation. Somehow, the cows weren't aware of this fact. This meant that my brothers were ceaselessly trying to show a herd of 40+ mature females exactly who was boss. However, the cows already knew who was boss, and it wasn't my brothers.

Let's face it; it's easy to see how trying to show a twelve-hundred-pound-animal that you're the boss can backfire. Cows may or may not be too bright, depending upon which side of the fence you stand on; but if you were the one sent out to pasture to bring the herd in and it didn't want to come, you'd soon discover that they can *run* really fast when they want to. Sometimes, they would run *away* from you, tails arched over their backs like the devil's own dog was hot on their heels. When that happened, it was best to simply stand your ground and not give chase; you could also hope that they'd stop running when they reached the fence. If they didn't, you'd have a real roundup on your hands. At other times, they might lower their heads and run *toward* you. At that point, the best course of action was to get out of the way. Such a moment was not, as you might imagine, a good time to stand your ground and try to reaffirm the whole 'who's boss' issue.

I also have two sisters. As mentioned, the older one would have rather died than work in the barn, which meant that I didn't get stuck doing dishes very often. This was a good thing, as I'd much rather have spent my time petting a cow than cleaning up a house–but that's a whole other article. My younger sister was the baby of the family. Being the only child at home after the rest of us left the nest, she ended up (through necessity) being good at everything–she could drive a tractor, milk cows, and clean the house with equal ease. I suppose there were times I envied her for that, for being so versatile–except for maybe the housework part.

As for myself, I was great with the animals, but not very good at the 'fieldwork' part of farming. My oldest memory of driving a tractor dates back to when I was very young. We had gone into the field to pick corn by hand, and I got to steer the old John Deere tractor because I was far too small to be much good at the 'picking' part. The tractor had a hand clutch–a long, metal handle you pulled back to make it stop and pushed ahead to make it go (or was it the other way around?) Granted, our progress was painfully slow and I spent most of the time sitting in the seat doing nothing, but every now and then I got to push the lever and turn the big steering wheel. That was fun.

When I got older, I graduated to the job of raking the hay. It was a good job for an incompetent tractor jockey. Unlike planting corn–which, if screwed up, would have all of the neighbors who drove by wondering what idiot had tried to plant corn in asymmetrical figure-eights–raking hay was hard to screw up. As I recall, that was when I learned the important lesson of never pushing the clutch in if you're raking hay and heading down hill! Boy, that hay was flying in all directions! I remember getting off the tractor at the bottom of the hill and trying to put the windrow back into a nice, straight row so Dad wouldn't know what had happened. I was too young to realize that such deception of a seasoned farmer like my father would have been impossible. My dad is so observant, he knows if someone has pulled in or out of their driveway while they're away–and he can tell you what type of vehicle they were driving, too. Knowing that, I now am certain that sad windrow of hay had 'blond, female driver' written all over it. Oh well, live and learn.

But the one thing I could never do to save my soul was back up a wagon. To this day, I'll drive around in a big loop rather than try it. I seem to remember there were large circles in the pasture where we unloaded the hay wagons. You see, if you parked too far away from the elevator, the bales wouldn't slide onto the chute correctly; and if you can't back the wagon up, your only choice was to drive all the way around and try again. I did just that–a lot. In the end, the hay got unloaded and the mow was filled. That was all that really mattered.

Today, I'm no better. I can't even back up my lawn mower with my little yard wagon hooked onto it. So I compensate for my lack of skill. I just jump off, unhook the wagon, get it pointed in whatever direction I need to go, and hook it back up. After that, I just climb back on and away I go. This may all sound stupid to those of you who have mastered the art of backing up a wagon, but we all have our talents and our shortcomings. Once someone knows what they can or can't do, the wise person adapts. Yes, we might circle around a few times trying to accomplish our goals, but sooner or later we get it right.

Someday

I have learned to hate the word 'someday'. Even when used in the context of hope, it pacifies us–luring us into a safe haven of inactivity. Someday I'll be thin, someday I'll balance the budget, someday the emptiness will all go away, someday I'll be happy . . . and the best part, or so we come to believe, is that all of this will happen with no effort on our part. All we have to do is wait and be patient, and one day it will show up on our doorstep, because that's the way it's meant to be.

In the presence of 'someday', time is an enemy. Days and years go by, dancing just beyond our grasp. We stand on the dock of life and watch them pass, one by one, a seemingly endless procession of ships laden with riches and treasures. We stare at them longingly, waiting for one of them to dock, yet all too soon they move off and are gone. They dip below the horizon, leaving us to remember just how close they had been–only yesterday. We sigh deeply and shrug off the loss. Perhaps they will return, someday.

Whenever possible, maybe we should replace the world 'someday' with 'today', or next week, or in one month–but a definite date, one that can be planned around and actually lived. I will balance the budget on the 30th. I will start dieting and keeping a food journal on the 1st of August. I will visit the library next Friday and check out some books on self-awareness. I will ask myself why I'm unhappy and I will listen quietly for the answers, even if I really don't want to hear them. And I will do it today. I'll start today.

When it's all said and done, we just can't afford to be 'someday' people, because someday may never come. It's fine to dream–in fact, it can be wonderful. But we have to act on those dreams. We have to break them down into smaller goals–tiny steps we can take to get us to where the dream lives. I am fond of a saying that reads, "How do you eat an elephant? One bite at a time." Of course, I wouldn't dream of eating an elephant, but it reminds me of an important lesson. Any task I face, even a seemingly impossible one, can be broken down into smaller tasks, ones I *can* handle. And the nicest thing about smaller tasks is they can be done today, not someday.

So think about it; give yourself a week or two. Watch and see how many times you can catch yourself playing the 'someday' game. Then, replace 'someday' with a real day–one you can mark down on the calendar and actually plan on. Maybe, with a little practice, we can retire the word 'someday'. We can tuck it away in a box with other phrases like 'riding off into the sunset', and 'happily ever after.' They are things that will never come to pass, unless you're willing to put forth the effort to make them real. It may well happen–if not today, possibly tomorrow. But it will never happen 'someday.'

Tapestries

We go through life trying to make sense of it all. We question, and worry, and wonder. But mostly, we find ourselves asking 'why'. It isn't the good times that are confusing. When good things happen, we tend to take them in stride and believe that life owes them to us. We expect good things to happen. We expect to fall in love someday, buy a house, raise a family, and perhaps travel when we retire. We somehow feel that such blessings are the rewards we receive for simply managing to stay alive. We can handle happiness, without question or hesitation. It is the sorrow we encounter that can bring us to our knees.

There we are, sailing through life, tending to our business, when it happens–a family member dies, a friend turns away, a loved one is unfaithful, a cherished pet disappears; from out of the blue, something painful finds us. And it really doesn't seem to matter if it's a sudden tragedy, or a loss you've seen coming for a very long time. The pain is intense and instantaneous. Often, the sorrow is followed by feelings of anger and frustration. We want to know 'why', and we want to know now! When the answers don't come, we falter and lose faith. We can't understand why life has to hurt. What did we do to deserve such sorrow? What could we have done to avoid such pain?

I don't have the answers . . . no one does. But several years back, I read an article that offered this theory. It spoke of life as being a vast tapestry–so large that we cannot see how the threads are interwoven. As we live our lives, we weave the colors–back and forth. Blind to the pattern, we live to create the wonder that is our life's tale. Sorrow and joy, fear and expectation–each emotion lends its own color to the scheme, completing the pattern only our Maker can see. We must struggle and weave, unaware of the glorious picture unfolding around us–trusting that, in the end, everything will be clear.

This past year has been a very colorful year for me, perhaps for you as well. I don't know what color sorrow or fear might yield in my tapestry–or joy either, for that matter, but I do know that it's time for me to switch skeins. With the holidays and their festivities lying ahead, I ask you to take time to remember the past year's joys and sorrows, gains and losses. Sigh if you must, or give thanks for a wonderful year if you were so blessed–but don't ever give in to doubt, and don't ever stop weaving. No one can complete your tapestry but you–and there's so much more 'life' just waiting to be spun.

To Memories and Future Walks

On June 22nd, I went with my daughter to have her dog put to sleep. He was a magnificent animal, only five years old; a dog with class and style. A Rottweiler by fate, Max had the heart of a lamb and the power of a lion. Bone cancer stole what would have been many more good years. Sometimes, tragedy strikes and we don't understand why.

Max, and his playmate Noah, had been living with me since last October. I took them in when my daughter and her husband found themselves moving from a house into an apartment, and the dogs could not go with them. They were not the burden I thought they would be. We put up a large 'kennel' in the back yard, complete with an insulated doghouse and a tarp for shelter on cold, wet days. All through the winter, I took them out on what I referred to as 'rott trots', which boiled down to extended walks with one end of a chain bound about my waist and the other end fastened around Max's neck. Noah followed freely, frolicking in the brisk, cold air. On these walks, I discovered the beauty of the woods when the snow was deep and crisp. We'd follow the frozen creek to the river and flush wild turkeys from the branches overhead. Footprints in the snow showed us where deer and rabbits had passed through. The whole world was a winter playground. I had no way of knowing then that it would be the only winter we would share.

Now it's summer, and there's only Noah in the large kennel that we built for her and her companion. Although we still take our walks, it isn't the same. A half an hour spent with me still leaves 23 ½ hours she spends each day all alone in her great big pen. When I put *my* dogs, Puddy and Toby, in with her, they only pout in the corner of the cage, wondering why they're being punished with confinement. They won't play, and they certainly aren't much company.

So I did something this last weekend that I've always wanted to do. I adopted a homeless animal from a shelter. It was every bit the wonderful experience I thought it would be. When they brought him out through the tempered glass door, it was love at first sight. Suddenly, I wasn't doing it just for Noah; I was doing it for me. He was 5-7 months old, a collie mix, and extremely sweet and timid. From 'borrowed time' in the back room of a vet's office, 'Grizzley' came to live with a loving family on a nice country lot. The workers at the Town and Country Vet Clinic were cheering because Grizzley found a home. Still, as thrilled as I am to have him, I can't forget that there are other dogs there waiting for their chance–two black labs, an adult female and a puppy. Surely someone has room for them, too . . . in their homes and in their hearts.

Pets are wonderful beings with whom we share our lives, but with them comes commitment and responsibility. They are yours for the whole trip. I can't kid myself–I know I've really adopted another heartache in disguise. At some point, all puppies grow old–or some other tragedy steps in to take them away. But people who share their lives with animals realize the benefits far outweigh the pain of saying goodbye. Another dog cannot take Max's place; that was not my intent. But Grizzley can make a place of his own. People who have known the love and devotion of a pet also know that the fields of the heart are large and fertile. Where pain and loss are buried, new joy and love can also grow. And there is more room there than we could ever know.

On Being in Love

Life has been kind enough in recent months to once again show me what it's like to be in love. I had long since forgotten the simple thrill of holding someone's hand as we'd walk from the car to the grocery store, or the crazy way your heart can skip a beat when someone simply smiles at you. I was no longer accustomed to shopping with a menu in mind that wasn't based on peanut butter, chicken nuggets, and extra-crispy frozen french fries. In a blink, it had all changed. "I" became "we", "mine" became "ours"; and for the first time in a long time, there was someone to consult with when making plans and decisions. I didn't have to do it all alone.

There was talk of vacations we could take and goals we could strive for; talk of how to spend our first Christmas, and all the Christmases to follow. I had a helping hand in taming the tomatoes that were threatening to take over the garden; and a partner to make salsa with on hot August afternoons. He shared my love of Victorian houses, and would not have dreamt of telling me that something 'couldn't be done'. In a heartbeat, my life had changed. There was someone there–someone mowing the lawn while I did the dishes, someone tinkering in the garage while I folded the clothes. My life began to center around the 'little things'–all the little things that make life so complete. There was someone to touch, someone to reassure me, someone to simply care.

But life holds no guarantees, and as suddenly as it had begun, it was gone. Yes, there was pain, and the overwhelming sensation that the bottom was once again dropping out of my world and carrying me with it. But seasoned lovers realize that the world doesn't end with a slamming door–or even with one that quietly clicks shut with all the finality of a tomb. It is, after all, a matter of perspective. Yes, life has, perhaps, been cruel; but it has also been honest enough to remind me how quickly my life can change. I'll admit it; I enjoyed having love momentarily brush up against my life, bringing with it all of the reminders of why it is such a grand part of us. And, despite the pain, I have no regrets. Broken hearts at the age of forty-three aren't nearly as bad as they were at seventeen. I know for a fact that the sun will rise again, even if I'm not particularly anxious to see it do so. At this age, there are too many things I need to be tending to–work, household chores, raising my son; I can't sit around wasting my time wondering about what might have been. I choose to overcome the whole thing by accepting that broken hearts are portable. I simply carry it with me wherever I go–an invisible weight that sometimes numbs my senses and slows my steps, but I don't stop living. That's another advantage of growing older; I've been here before. I know, for certain, that the show must go on.

Life is far too short. We can't afford to waste time being cynical. Love, with all of its challenges and risks, is still the only game in town. If, by chance, we are lucky enough to find that certain someone, we need to love them unconditionally, and believe in all that we can be. That's the easy part–the 'fun' part. The hard part is that we need to do that and still be aware of the risk we are taking. There are no guarantees. That's just how the game is played–it's all or nothing. Still, as Alfred Lord Tennyson wrote long ago, "I hold it true, whate'er befall; I feel it, when I sorrow most; 'Tis better to have loved and lost than never to have loved at all."

Round Two

There is much literature written on love. It has been the topic of poets' musings and songwriters' works for thousands of years. I, myself, have this to say. Those authors and artists who celebrate the condition of being "young and in love" are missing the big picture. If you truly want romance and passion and drama, try hammering out the challenges of joining two lives after the age of forty (or fifty) for that matter. Try learning the art of "sharing" when you've both been independent for far too long (and darn good at it, too, thank you very much!) Try balancing two lives, two households, two checkbooks (which soon becomes three–yours, mine and ours). Try meeting the challenges of having two sets of ex-in-laws, children, pets, and friends. Even the simplest words, such as "home", take on a whole new meaning. 'Whose' home? Which one? When you're going 'home' after being out, are you turning left or right at the next stop sign? It all depends on whose home is 'home' for that moment.

How much easier it is to be 'young' and in love. How simple to mold your life around another human being's when you really haven't established one of your own. At my age, everything is pretty well set–and settling. Even the simplest things become a test of 'how' things should be done. Take, for example, the refrigerator. Please don't come into my kitchen and move the eggs out of the door. That's where I keep them. I know they shouldn't be there (because it's the warmest part of the frig), but that's where Frigidaire installed the egg tray and that's where they're staying. And while we're on the topic of household chores, no, I don't want to learn a 'better' way to fold my towels–and how on earth did the dish soap end up resting on the workbench in the garage? What do you mean it wasn't you who moved it? Did it grow legs and walk?

After a brief 'hiatus', John and I have decided to give our relationship another try. Ultimately, I guess we decided that living apart was harder than living together and making the effort to overlook our differences. At our age (middle age), it's all about compromise–and what we choose not to change we at least have to understand. Seeing life through another's eyes has opened up a whole new world for me. For the first time in many years, I've learned that it's okay to be weak. In fact, I now know that *not* being perfect makes me even more lovable–at least to him. This time, we're actually making it work, despite the fact that we're both perfectionists (of

German descent) who are far too stubborn to joyfully give even an inch.

But even the lives of two middle-age German perfectionists can be blended together. To do so, we just have to respect who the other person is, and accept where he/she has been. That can be a tall order to fill. At our age, we may well have more past lying behind us than we have future stretching out ahead. The past, and its memories, are fragile, treasured things. Falling in love later in life is accepting everything about one another–past and present. It is also realizing that there are some details about the other person's life that they may never be able to share. At our age, we are not the "first" anything. We're not each other's first love, first spouse, first heartache, first challenge, first partner, or first friend. Still, in spite of all of this, we can still become 'first' in each other's life. We can be the person they first think of, the person they first turn to, and the person they first miss when we are away. Love is better at this age than any other age. Let the young lovers fill the streets, hand in hand, en route to their first kiss, first love, first passion. Those things will pass. Instead, show me an older couple that has found each other in the afternoon of their lives. At this age, we're old enough and wise enough to know what we've found, and not young enough or foolish enough to ever let it go.

Cabooses

Call me old-fashioned if you like, but it doesn't seem right that there is no longer a caboose at the end of every train. When I am stranded at a railroad crossing, waiting for the train to finish passing, I still look for that boxy, little car with its tapered roof and a man sitting in its window–but there is only an empty coupling where the caboose used to be.

The caboose has a colorful history. It first came into being in the 1840's on the famed New York Railway. At that time, it was a simple wooden box built on a flatbed railroad car. It was where the crew rested and ate and stowed their gear. In fact, the word "caboose" comes from the word "cambose," which is a French nautical term for a house built on the deck of a ship that served the same purpose. Aside from providing comfort, the caboose served as a lookout point and a means by which the two ends of the train communicated, which was particularly useful when the train was backing up. Someone riding in the caboose could keep a watchful eye on the cars moving along the track between him and the engine, and he would signal the engineer if he felt there was a problem. Switchmen, brakemen and flagmen were stationed in the caboose. It was their job to work the switch in the track that changed the train's course, as well as to aid in hooking up new railroad cars and disconnecting old ones.

Today, modern technology has eliminated the need for the caboose. The switches that change the train's course are now electronic, and cars are added and released with greater ease. Because of this, Alaska is the only state that still utilizes cabooses on its trains–and even there the caboose's future is tentative at best. On the bright side, 'decommissioned' cabooses have become a hot item. Collectors are rallying to purchase them, after which they are used for roadside coffee stands, storage sheds and cabins. One web site reported that they were going for $12,000 to $14,000 each. That sounds like a lot of money for an item that averages 14 ft. high and 41 ft. long. Still, the trick may not be in buying a caboose, but rather in moving it. Weighing in at 52,000 pounds–without the wheels and undercarriage–you better be sure you know where you're going to put it, because that's where it's going to stay.

I suppose it would be kind of romantic to have a caboose in one's yard. You could build a white picket fence around it and place flower boxes in its windows. But for me, at least, it just wouldn't be the same. For me, that caboose was part of a train and that's where it belongs. I can still close my eyes and see it moving off down the track, swaying gently from side to side. And while the engine amazed me with its brawn and power, the caboose charmed me by simply bringing up the end. Without it, the train is not complete. What was the harm in leaving it in place–in allowing it to mark the end of the train for decades to come? There are far worse things in this country that are allowed to simply "go along for the ride."

The Story Behind the Song

My home is in the perfect location for bird-watching. I own a big open field, surrounded on three sides by forest, and the variety of birds that flock to my feeders is truly amazing. During the day, I have the chickadees and the goldfinches, the doves and the blue jays. Now and then, a rose-breasted grosbeak happens along, and phoebes can be heard calling from the treetops. An occasional indigo bunting can be seen perched on the trellis outside my kitchen window, and hummingbirds stream back and forth from the feeder to some hidden nest. In the winter, flocks of dark-eyed juncos search for food in my backyard as several pairs of cardinals watch from nearby branches. It all seems so tranquil . . .

But, about a week ago, a new song awakened me. At some point, after trying more than once to go back to sleep, I realized that the bird wasn't about to let that happen. Stumbling out of bed, I made my way to the kitchen, intent on making the morning coffee. The song seemed even louder in that room and my sleepy eyes searched the world outside my window, trying to pinpoint its source. It took a while, but I finally found it.

A few weeks back, I had erected an arched, garden gate not far from my house. There, perched on the top of the arch, was a tiny brown bird with a very loud mouth. I got out my worn copy of *Guide to Birds* and quickly learned that my new alarm clock was nothing more than a common house wren. As his song filled the room, I chuckled at what the book had to say about his life.

He was described as 'an energetic bird, with a loud song.' Yup, they got that part right. The Chippewas named him "O-du-na-mis-sug-ud-da-we'-shi", which means 'a big noise for its size.' While this all seemed both accurate and interesting, the amusing part was yet to come. The book went on to say that the male is the first to arrive at his summer home. Once there, he stakes out his territory and starts building several nests by stuffing any likely site with grass and twigs. When the female arrives and the courtship begins, he takes her on a tour of his proposed nesting sites. While she eventually approves of one of the 'sites', she rejects his attempt at nest building and scatters his twigs about. She wants it built *her* way. I smiled and read on.

According to the authors of *Guide to Birds,* domestic battles often rage and, while the female works on the new nest, the male starts a second one nearby–which will eventually be used for a different brood with a new 'wife' (and we humans think we're the only ones with relationship problems!) So the next time you're enjoying the soothing sound of a bird singing at the top of his lungs, don't assume he sings because he's happy. In reality, if the song is coming from a common house wren, he may well be telling his first wife exactly where she can put those new twigs.

The Roads We Take

You just have to love the roads in Wisconsin when February rolls around. The salt, the sand, the ice, the potholes–they are all part of daily life if you live in this great state and the calendar is caught between the dead of winter and approaching spring. Two months ago, the Hogsback Road on which I live was a smooth ribbon of blacktop (neatly concealed beneath an inch of solid ice) that uneventfully led me wherever I needed to go. Today, it's a commuting challenge–a collection of ridges, and dips, and random lapses of pavement that is intent on destroying my little car, one jolt and bump at a time.

This is not surprising. Winter roads are just one of the many things (like blizzards, sub-zero temperatures, and the Packers failing to make it to the Super Bowl yet again) that we have to contend with here in Wisconsin between Christmas and Easter. We learn to deal with it. Like so many other drivers, I slow down for the bumps and the patches of ice, and I try to successfully weave in and out among the potholes. Such maneuvers force me to drive a little slower than usual. This, in turn, gives me more time to think . . .

As a result of those moments of deep contemplation (combined with an overly active imagination), I have come to believe that roads in Wisconsin in February are a lot like life. In life, for the most part, we all travel along and experience a fairly good trip. During most stages of our lives, our 'cars' roll along without much trouble. Oh, there may be an occasional rainstorm, maybe even some hail, and areas of construction are around every bend; but, our journeys continue on with little or no trouble. We make our plans, pack our suitcases, fill our gas tanks, and head out for parts unknown; and, through it all, we take the 'road' for granted. It's there to serve us.

Then, without warning, it happens. The roads we travel daily suddenly take on new forms. The bumps arrive, and there are dips, ridges, and potholes everywhere. We get angry. They slow us down. They weren't there yesterday, and we certainly don't want them there today. In fact, we want them gone! To make matters worse, they're more than just a nuisance; they can cause some real damage. They can knock us out of alignment and threaten to throw us off course. They demand our attention and refuse to be ignored. They force us to hit the breaks when we want to hit the gas.

Whether it's the roads we're commuting on or the lives we're living, the story is pretty much the same. Just when we get comfortable, fate throws us some curves. We get angry, in part, because the curves slow us down. We hadn't included them in our plans, and we most certainly don't want to deal with them. Indeed, they confuse us; things were going along so well, why did the potholes have to appear? Why do bills pile up, why do friends become distant, why do jobs fade away? The answer is a simple one, and it's the same for all of us. The answer is simply, 'that's life'. If things were always easy, we'd never have to grow. If the sun were always shining, there'd never be a rainbow at the back edge of a storm. If roads were always straight and clear, we might be tempted to drive too fast and lose our way. Sometimes, we need a pothole to force us to change direction. Sometimes we need that bump (or two) to slow us down. It's not the end of the world–or even the end of the road. If we learn to just slow down a bit, have faith, and give it some time, we will realize that problems can be just like our roads in late winter. Sooner or later, they'll smooth themselves out.

Registration Time

Computers have indisputably earned their place as a modern wonder. They make our lives easier, and surround us in each and every part of our lives. In our homes, they allow us to send emails, pay bills, and surf the web. Outside our doors in the public domain, they are used by virtually every business, agency, and organization. They keep records, track sales, print statements, run programs, record inventory, and manage budgets; they do it all. But computers also fill another niche. They play an important role that will never be discussed in staff meetings, or mentioned in the fine print of a software marketing plan. This unique role they fill isn't in the form of a program, and it doesn't need to be updated. As a matter of fact, computers are capable of this handy little trick without even being turned on. That unique trick is this–they are there to take the blame.

Ever get charged too much at a store? It was the computer's fault–it didn't scan the item properly. Ever have a monthly statement from your credit card arrive with a mistake on it? Who did the company blame, or are they still arguing it can't be a mistake because computers are never wrong? I studied computer programming in college years ago. One of the first things the class emphasized was the term, "Garbage in, garbage out." This phrase captures the fact that computers can only work with the info they're given, good or bad. Enough said.

Now, I'll confess that I'm writing this because I have an ax to grind with the Wisconsin DMV. I'm about to write a letter to them and I thought it might be a good idea to let off some steam first. Here's the scenario. My car registration is due at the end of April. I've owned this car since 1997. Since that time, I've never moved and, in doing so, taken the car with me. In other words, the car has always been registered in Oconto County and kept in the township of Little River. She's always been parked in my garage on the Hogsback Road. Always.

In 2002, for the first time since purchasing the car, I didn't receive my registration notice–that little blue and white postcard that you're supposed to mail back with the appropriate fee. I wrongly blamed the postal service. (Sorry, guys!) To remedy the problem, I visited the DMV online and printed out the form they have on file there–the one you're supposed to use if you don't get your renewal notice (sounds like this is a common occurrence) or if you get it and lose it (who, me?). Anyway, I printed the form out and filled in the blanks. It was basic stuff like my name, address, etc.–and of course, don't forget to enclose the check. I got my stickers . . . eventually. Better late than never, right? They were mailed to me at my correct address. No problem there. I assumed that, whatever the mix-up had been, it was now corrected.

Shortly after I'd logged on and corrected the problem, my ex-husband had come over with a little blue and white postcard in his hand. "Since when does your registration notice come to me?" he'd asked. Sure enough, there it was. *My* notice had been sent to his house–and no, it wasn't a mistake on the mailman's part. Apparently I had moved in with my ex-husband in the township of Pensaukee–and, in moving there, I had apparently taken the car with me.

Where, I wondered, did the DMV get this information from? How can they change a person's address and what township a vehicle is kept in without being told to? Oh yes, I know how–it was one of those damn computers, that's what it was; that's what did it! It was all due to a small misdirection of information. I crumpled the card and threw it away. After all, I'd entered the correct (and unchanged) information when I'd visited the DMV's web site, so the ordeal was supposedly behind me. Right?

Wrong. Five years have passed since my registration notice was (mistakenly?) first sent to my ex-husband's house, and in each consecutive year since, it's been sent there again. I've crossed out the information on the card that requests where the vehicle is being kept; I've 'lined through' the address and entered my own. Nothing seems to matter. The DMV is apparently convinced that my car resides in Pensaukee with my ex, and I'm getting too frustrated (and tired) to argue with them.

I suppose I'm making a big deal out of nothing, but you can't help but wonder how the whole system works. Again this year I will compose and send my letter, and next year, undoubtedly, the card will get sent to the same place. I can, at that point, either wait for my ex to cough it up or I can go online yet again to take care of the matter. I suppose worse things could have happened, especially when we're discussing the government and my personal information that is currently being stored in their files. But I *will* say this; if the DMV suddenly decides that I've moved in with Mel Gibson (and taken my little Aspire with me) I won't bother making any changes on *that* card. After all, if the system malfunctions to your advantage, you might as well enjoy it while it lasts!

Once Upon A Small Family Farm . . .

I saw an interesting story on the news the other night. It seems some residents of Calumet County, Wisconsin, are voicing their opposition to a 'mega-farm' being built there. The proposed farm will be home to 3000+ cows, and the residents are concerned about what that will do to their quality of life. They're worried about possible ground water contamination, and of course, with that many animals, there is always the question of where you draw the line on 'fresh country air.'

I find it hard to imagine a farm with that many cows. Growing up, on a small, family farm, we had our hands full taking care of forty-four lactating mothers. But farms, like most other businesses, have been forced to grow to stay competitive. Rising feed costs and the skyrocketing overhead of fuel prices and interest rates, coupled with falling milk prices, have made farming more challenging, if not impossible. A farmer buying a new tractor today will pay two or three times what my father paid for an entire farm back in 1957. That kind of debt has changed the approach to 'successful farming'. Instead of being a 'way of life' that people practice to be self-sufficient and raise a family, it has morphed into a business with hourly employees and tax withholding.

Not all farmers have made the change. A lot of them found themselves at the age of retirement when this metamorphosis hit. Their children, hard-working individuals who were educated far beyond their parents' level, chose careers with 40-hour work weeks and no midnight calvings to deal with. Proud farmers, who had dedicated their lives to working the land, found that there was no one 'waiting in the wings' to take over their livelihood. A dream ended; life moved on.

A person need only take a short drive through the countryside to witness the outcome of these changes. Everywhere, there are aging barns standing empty, and hay fields dotted with crops of new houses instead of corn or wheat. Heirless farmers, or those whose families have simply decided to call it quits, are moving on and selling out. The result of this is that land that once fed the farmers' herds is being bought up by two separate groups–private individuals who want that special 'home in the country', and mega-farms. And those two parties do not necessarily want to live on the same 'country' block, even if it is a mile long.

This, I suppose, brings me back to the debate in Calumet County. I can understand the concerns being voiced, but I don't think the establishment of a mega-farm there will be stopped. 'Progress' seldom is. It may be delayed, but it's never stopped. The massive free-stall barns that would be needed to house 3000+ animals may not be built this year, but they will be built. It's only a matter of time.

For those who, like me, mourn the passing of the small, family farm, I suppose it shouldn't matter if the milk we drink or the butter we use comes from a 'mega' farm, or a small family operation. After all, keeping the prices down for the consumer should always be our first concern, shouldn't it? Still, the disappearance of the 'small family farm' pains me deeply. I believe that it is the end of an era that formed the very basis of this country. It was a good life, held together by hard work and discipline. Those of us who were fortunate enough to be raised on such a farm knew of responsibility and commitment; we learned of sacrifice, and of life and death. Every lesson life could offer was woven into our daily schedule, one season at a time. We worked together. We pulled together. Then, as now, farming was a way of life, not a job or a career. There were no paid holidays, no overtime, and we worked just as hard on Sundays as any other day of the week.

On a small farm, the cows all had names. You knew them, each from the other, because you'd raised their mothers, and their grandmothers, and many of their sisters. And each one was different, with its own personality and its own quirks. The chore of 'milking' was done best by those who knew each and every animal. Some cows milked out fast, some slow. Some milked faster on three quarters than they did on the fourth. Some would kick the milker off the second they were done, on some it would have to hang forever. Knowing these things made your job a little easier, but they were not the only things you needed to know.

For instance, you learned to always close the pasture gate. If you forgot and the cows got out, they would scatter in all directions, bouncing through the knee-high cornfields like the spring chickens that they most definitely were not. You'd run, panting, behind them, as they kicked up clods of dirt and galloped on ahead with their tails curled up over their backs. You also learned that threatening storm clouds meant that the wagons of hay had to be unloaded fast–really fast; and calves were always born when there was a wedding or party the family was obligated to attend.

There were no milking parlors back then. Each cow had its own spot in the barn; you went to her when it was milking time; she didn't come to you. Moving between the cows, morning and night, time and again, you discovered that their tails were quick, and usually dirty, and their tongues were long and rough. You learned that they, and life, were unpredictable–but well worth the time spent on both.

I guess that, in today's economy, the mega-farm may well be the only way to farm that makes any financial sense–but at what cost? I know that we are losing something very special as night falls and the lights go out for the final time in yet another small barn somewhere in Wisconsin (or Iowa, or Minnesota, or anywhere in America). Those farms, and their families, have held us together and tied us to this earth. They were the roots that made the American people strong. Their lifestyle taught us of hard work, and commitment, and striving together as a family toward common goals. When the chores were all done in the evening and the cows were settling down in their stalls, I remember feeling that it had been a good day, and that all was right with the world. Back then, when I myself lived on a small family farm, life was good–hard, but simple–and tomorrow was just a sunrise away.

A Measure of Worth

I've been working at restoring a 1966 Chevy pickup. Early on in the project, I learned that a truck has a great many parts (and that mine would need many of them replaced to bring her back to her original condition.) At this early stage of the project, she's got three things going for her (yes, it's a 'she'.) The first thing is that, when you turn the key and patiently work the gas pedal, she starts. The second thing is that, when you shift through the gears, she moves. The third good thing is that, when you step on the brakes, she stops. That's very important. Of course, seeing that she's currently balanced on four blocks of wood in my garage, she's not doing any of those things right now. She's basically just sitting there, in a comical state of partial disassembly, waiting for all the bolts and her various pieces and parts to be put back in place and tightened down.

Working on Cassie–what self-respecting truck doesn't have a name?–gives me lots of time to reflect on life. As I'm searching for the right size wrench, or wondering where I placed that missing bolt, my mind wanders. For instance, I find myself thinking about the truck's past owners. Based on a faded "Rent a Wreck, Appleton, WI", bumper sticker crookedly placed on her back end, I am relatively certain that her past is a colorful one. What roads has she travelled down? What conversations has she overheard? What eventually led her to be parked on the side of Highway 41 with a faded "For Sale" sign propped in her window?

This particular truck had been for sale for a couple of months before I'd finally stopped to take a closer look. Like me, countless people had driven past her, day after day, probably with little more than a quick glance. Had I not eventually stopped and purchased her, someone else may well have decided she was worth a closer look. If not, the owner would have finally been forced to remove her from her spot at the side of the road and give up trying to make a sale. At that point, he may have taken on the restoration project himself, or he may have parked her back behind the barn and earmarked her as a 'someday' project. Eventually, she may have been towed to a junkyard, stripped for parts and sold as scrap metal. Her future was a crapshoot, with no guarantees.

In many ways, our lives are just like an old truck that's been parked on the side of the road with a colorful "For Sale" sign propped up in its window. With the two exceptions of death and taxes, we have no guarantees that someone will eventually buy us, repair our fenders, sand off the rust, and apply some fresh paint. There is no assured outcome for each of our lives, and no set path has been laid out before us like some newly-blacktopped road. I had simply been driving to work when I happened to see the old truck sitting in that hayfield by the side of the road. Had she been parked somewhere else, I wouldn't have seen her at all; had I been someone else, I might not have stopped. As it turned out, she's sitting safely in my garage, denying the junkyard its 'just due'. The truck's fate, like our own, was all a matter of chance; it depended on how the cards played out.

Think about it for a moment, if you will; ponder all of the 'what ifs' we could ask about our lives. What if I'd been born somewhere else, what if I'd lived my life in a different time, what if I'd been thin, or rich, or tall, or famous? These are questions that can never be answered, but that doesn't stop us from considering them. And yet, in spite of the thousands of possibilities and all of the ways our lives could have been different, there is one thing that I believe. We are all exactly where we're supposed to be. Oh, we might not like it. We might even envy others for their wealth, or for the apparent lack of trouble in their lives. We might even dismiss our shortcomings by claiming that luck just wasn't with us, or that we're victims of fate and circumstance.

Sure, there's luck involved in life–both good and bad. And yes, some of us may have gotten a little more 'help' than others (or a lot). At one point, someone thought enough of Cassie to drop a 327 V-8 engine in her. Thank you very kindly! But we can't simply wait for someone to make the necessary changes for us.

There is nothing stopping us except *us*. I've heard it said that you can choose to curse the darkness, or you can light a single candle to show the way. Your destiny is your own. You choose. At times, I think we're all 'Cassies', sitting at the side of the road, hoping someone will come along, take us in, and fix all our worn-out parts. But there's one major difference between an old truck and us. The 'key' to our lives is not taped to the underside of a fender; or resting, forgotten, in the bottom of a soiled ashtray. It's in our hands. Maybe it's time to fire up the old engine, burn out the carbon, and run through the gears. In life, unlike in the 'real' world, there are no speed limits–unless you choose to set some–and there really is nothing to hold you back.

Just please make sure that all your fenders are securely bolted in place before heading out.

Retirement and Heaven

There are many things in life that people look forward to, but two of the biggest ones that come to mind are vacations and retirement. Some people like to spend their vacations traveling. They want to see the world, experience different cultures, sample exotic foods, or just get away from it all. Perhaps they want to visit the Grand Canyon, or sleep in the shadows of the great Rocky Mountains. For some people, this is what vacation is all about–getting away. For me, my favorite kind of vacation is one I get to spend at home, working about the yard or tackling a major project. That way, I feel like I've accomplished something with my time off from work, and I usually saved some money to boot.

If we're lucky, there comes a day when vacations are obsolete. That time in our life is called retirement. Oh, retired people still travel and set out to see the world, but they don't have to take time off from work to do it; so technically, it's not a 'vacation'. I think about retirement now and then, and I have a hunch that I'll think about it a lot more as I grow older. It's kind of funny, but I'm not entirely sold on the concept. You see, if retirement is your chance to take it easy after having worked your entire life, I don't think that I'll be very good at it.

For one thing, I tend to work harder on my days off than I do at work. From mowing the lawn, to creating stone and concrete steps and walks, to upholstering furniture or occasionally hanging a sheet of drywall, I often have to return to work just to recuperate–and that's really sad. Besides, I enjoy having a routine. Oh sure, I complain when the alarm clock goes off at 5 a.m., or when I have to put in overtime on the job; but, all in all, I enjoy working, and being part of a team, and offering some support. I guess it all boils down to the fact that I need a reason to get up in the morning–one that can't be put off indefinitely. Retirement, to me, seems to be a real quick way to get old fast. But, who knows? Maybe I'll change my mind when I get there.

While I'm on the topic of life's 'long-term' rewards, I might as well confess that I have a really quirky view on heaven as well. I never could buy in to that 'living among the clouds' theory. You know the one I'm talking about, complete with harps and iridescent wings. At one point in my life, I did buy into the idea that heaven would be like a huge resort–one where everything and everyone who had lived a good life could just hang out forever. No harps or wings, just a lot of time to kick back and be happy.

But to be honest, I'm just not sure; and the fact that nobody else seems to be real clear on the issue isn't exactly reassuring. The main problem I have with an eternity floating in the clouds is this: humans enjoy being challenged. *I* enjoy being challenged. Peace on earth, harmony, no more pain and suffering–these are truly wonderful things that we should aspire to. But, as good as that all sounds, wouldn't it start getting old after awhile? I mean, think about it–you wouldn't be needed, you wouldn't be helpful, and there wouldn't be one single thing that you'd 'have' to do. I can't imagine not accomplishing something in a month, let alone for an eternity. I'd go bonkers! Sure, I'd like to see my loved ones who've gone on before me, but once you've filled them in on everything they've missed, what would there be left to talk about? The Packers? God forbid there'd be sports up there (which is a whole other topic!)

So, I'm stuck in limbo about what waits on the 'other side', as well as where I'll spend my next vacation–and, I'm really in no hurry to find out either one. Whatever–or wherever–it is, I'll have to trust that it's going to be good. After all, vacations come and go, just like the years; and, as for heaven, no one's ever come back to complain.

Child Support

A woman I work with recently received a child support check in the amount of six cents. Amused by the stupidity of the whole deal, she toyed with the thought of having a friend follow her to the bank with a video camera. Once there, she was going to deposit two cents in her first son's college fund, another two cents in the second son's account, and then she was going to ask for the balance in cash to try and buy groceries on her way home. As one would expect, she received another support check a short time later for the correct amount (minus the six cents).

I shake my head; so this is what the world has come to. For one thing, it is tragic that the state even needs a system to collect and distribute child support. I suppose it sprang from the fact that, years ago, too many single parents (mostly women, but a few men) were forced to seek out welfare in order to prevent their children from going hungry. To offset the financial drain, the state set up a system by which absent parents were made accountable (financially, at least) for the offspring they'd brought into this world, and then abandoned. Over the years, the system has grown and become more complex. Today, with the help of computerized technology, the absentee parent is tracked by his/her social security number. Wages are then garnished, and tax refunds and lottery winnings are seized–all to ensure that the children are provided for.

Don't get me wrong; I'm not against child support being paid or received. I have some first-hand knowledge of what it takes to raise a child (which, by the way, is a whole lot more than money!) What I'm against is the need for a 'child support system'. How can parents, men or women, turn their backs on their own children? And, while we're at it, if someone has no intention of loving and raising a child, why do they even bother bringing one into the world?

For many years, 'freedom of choice' has been a 'hot' topic. I absolutely believe we have the freedom to choose, but that freedom starts a whole lot sooner than after the first missed period. We can choose a career, a college, and a town to call home. We can choose to remain single or get married. Someday, we may have children (hopefully, it is by choice). This is all well and good; however, people are abusing this freedom by choosing to plunge into relationships with little or no intention of making a true commitment. Then, when the relationship fails, it is the children who pay the price. Yes, people change and 'things' happen. Not every marriage or commitment has a happy ending; life doesn't work that way. But your child is still your child, no matter where, or with whom, they may be currently living.

This world is far from perfect; and, because people don't 'choose' to act responsibly, we have a child support system that steps in and forces them to. As the number of irresponsible people has grown, the system has also grown, becoming so complex that it can't hope to be efficient. As my friend can testify, we now have computers spitting out support checks in the amount of six cents; the check is literally not worth the paper it's printed on, let alone the postage that was spent to mail it out.

There is no easy solution to this growing problem of supporting our children; no simple answer dances just outside our grasp. We can't magically create a world where families stay together; nor can we attempt to restructure a government program so that it contains at least a grain of common sense. The situation has spun so far out of control, that there really is no easy cure. Do we change people's priorities so the system is no longer necessary, or do we attempt to change the system itself? Either task would be an uphill battle with little chance of success. At least, that's my opinion–and it's a full six cents' worth.

One Year Older

According to the date that's printed on both my driver's license and my birth certificate, I'm one year older today than I was yesterday. But that's not true, not really. I'm actually only one *day* older than yesterday, but who's counting, right?

I've never cared too much for birthdays. Not only am I intimidated by the thought of growing older, I really don't like all the fuss and the bother that goes hand-in-hand with the occasion. The presents, the cake, the 'blowing out' of the candles (yes, they still make me do that!)–it's all a lot of hoopla for something that most people would rather avoid as the years unfold. Life is a 'catch twenty-two' situation that we all must deal with. No one wants to die young, yet no one wants to grow old. Then, just when we think that we can sneak our way past another birthday unnoticed, someone shoves a cake under our nose and starts singing about it!

I really can't complain. It's been a good year. I've grown older and wiser, and made some new friends. I even signed my first contract with a literary agent, who is now hard at work marketing my first novel. Above and beyond all of that, I've found someone who really loves me. He shares my passion for old houses and hard work, and he's not afraid to dream. Looking back, I'd say that's a damn, fine year for me to tuck away in my memoirs.

But each year that stretches out behind us leaves one less that lies ahead. Life seems unfair that way. The better we get at living, the less time we have to make it all work. Even the process of aging is deceiving. At one time in our lives, thirty seems old–until suddenly we're forty and thirty sounds like heaven. When we were in grade school, the high school seniors looked so mature; now, we watch them race out of the school parking lot in their beat-up cars and we wonder how these kids managed to get a driver's license.

Birthdays. They're unavoidable. In fact, they're a little like catching a cold–sooner or later, you know that one is going to find you. You can hide in bed and wait for it to go away, but that rarely ever works. In fact, experience has taught me that it's best to meet a birthday head-on. Make the most of it; indulge your family's need to watch you blow out the ever-increasing number of birthday candles–with one exception. If the candles are 'sparking' as they burn, don't even waste your time. No one is ever obligated to deal with trick candles that refuse to go out. In those situations, just slide the cake down to the children (or grandchildren) and let them have the honors. Aging, if it grants us nothing else, should have some dignity attached to it.

What's in *Your* Closet?

I have this impossible dream. I'd like my house to be straightened and organized. I'd like to know exactly what's in every drawer, and in every room, without looking. I'd like the canned soup to stop trespassing into the canned vegetables' territory; I'd like the towels to rest in the cupboard next to their appropriate washcloths; I'd like the sheets to all have matching pillowcases (that are clean at the same time); and I'd like the dryer to stop eating one half of every good pair of socks.

I'd like my house to be like the ones you see on TV–the ones where they have a cat (but there's no sign of a litter box), or they have a dog that comes into the house in every episode, but never punctuates his entrance by coughing up the grass he just ate in the backyard. In that house, when they open their closets, everything is piled neatly, color-coordinated, and never out of place. They don't seem to have clothes that fit last year, but may fit never again–let alone ones that waiting to come back in style. And what about the junk drawer–have you ever watched any show on TV where the family had a good junk drawer? I thought every household had at least *one* of them; at last count, I think I had three. Where else would I put spare batteries, shoe laces (from the shoes I pitched last year, but the laces were still fine), rubber bands, and the arm to the G.I. Joe doll that fell off and needs to get glued back on? It's in there, right next to the glue–now if I could just find the *rest* of the toy!

While this lack of organization on my part might be viewed by some as a type of sickness or 'condition', I know that's not true. In fact, there's a whole other side to this organization scenario. As proof, I once had a brother-in-law who arranged his canned goods alphabetically, and bought all white socks (same size, same brand), then marked the toes of the pairs with different colored threads so he'd always know which sock went with which. I don't think I'd ever want to go *that* far, if for no other reason than I would never have the time. Besides, it would be very confusing–would 'green beans' get arranged with the 'G's or the 'B's? And what would happen when you ate the last can of chili, would 'corn' get bumped up a space–or would you just leave that slot empty until the next time you went shopping?

No, I think I could be quite happy with much smaller accomplishments. I'd like people to no longer be able to write notes in the dust on my bookshelf–not that anyone in *my* family would ever dream of doing such a thing! I'd like the clean clothes to all get folded and put away (*before* I need the clothes basket again), and I'd like all of the dirty clothes to make it into the hamper on the first try, without taking the scenic route. And the toothpaste splatters on the bathroom mirror? I ought to either connect the dots to make a scenic picture, or seriously arm myself with a rag and some glass cleaner.

This all sounds so overwhelming! Perhaps I should just take it one step at a time. First, I'll make an effort to get all of the calendars in my house set to the same month; then I'll get all of the clocks set to the same time. When I think I'm ready, I'll take the *big* step. I'll give that G.I. Joe guy exactly one week to turn himself in, or the arm is history! Maybe, by Christmas next year, I'll have begun to make a dent.

In the Shadow of 9/11

Some time ago, on 9/11/2001, all of our lives changed–and not for the better. No longer do we, as a people, feel safe from terrorists, and we no longer assume that tragedy won't find us. We are no longer innocent, nor are we whole.

Immediately following the attack, the people of America rallied. We threw up a collective, defiant fist and shook it loudly, assuring the world that we could not be broken. Eventually, though, the dust had to settle and life had to go on, but it wasn't the same life. Now we're afraid and we don't want to admit it. Some of us won't leave the country, others won't fly at all. Our sons are fighting and dying. We watch the news, see the violence, and pray that it's not the start of World War III.

Our economy took a huge blow, stumbled and fell to its knees. Jobs were lost; companies folded. Many of us who had previously felt secure in our employment are now wondering what next year–or even next week–is going to bring. The sense of security that we had so taken for granted has been ripped out of our lives, and yes–we are afraid.

So now, some considerable time later, here we are. We're still struggling, still trying to recover, still missing the world we knew prior to the attack. I still listen to my son talk about his day when I pick him up from school, but I wonder more than ever what the future holds for him–and for all of our children. I hate the uncertainty. I hate not being able to believe things can be as they were. I hate not knowing if I'll have a job next month, or the same home in a year.

But yet, in the shadow of uncertainty, an amazing peace has found me. I know all things happen for a reason. I know that change is hard and that humans tend to resist it until they are thrown, kicking and screaming, into its waiting arms. We have to believe–now more than ever–that there was a reason for this tragedy. We have to look to the other side of our loss and strive to make the future better, despite our uncertainty and fear. In the weeks following 9/11, many experts were quoted as saying that, if Americans allowed themselves to be changed by the attack, then the terrorists would have won. The experts saw an importance in getting back to normal, a need to continue traveling–continue living–as we have always done. Indeed, the experts are right; we should strive to do so–and we are striving, we are trying. But while our lives should not change, our beliefs must. We can't believe in the way things used to be. Our strength is not in who we were before this tragedy. It is time to look ahead–and within. We need to believe in the future, in ourselves, in each other, and in Someone far greater.

Eighteen years ago, while she was still in grade school, my daughter made a picture and brought it home. She'd colored a squirrel and scribbled a short prayer next to it that the teacher had given her. I've said that prayer so often and now, more than ever, it comforts me and helps me deal with this strange, uncertain world. The prayer goes like this:

"God will provide for me, I know,

but I must do my part.

I must take care of what He gives,

and keep faith in my heart."

It's a simple thing I can do; take care of all that God places within my life. So I follow this prayer as best I can. I also strive to leave each place I pass through a little better than I found it. The hardest part may well be keeping the faith–especially today. But if our faith falters, they win; and we're not about to let that happen.

Parenting

For Christopher

It is a mother's job to worry, and we do it very well. I brought three children into this world, and I feel blessed in the fact that they were all born healthy and with a fair degree of intelligence, which they use from time to time. But it was always their level of compassion that brought me more joy than the A's and B's that came home on their quarterly report cards. My two daughters came into my life when I was very young, so they are now grown and 'out of the nest'. I see them almost every weekend. Once my children, they are now my friends and confidants. They bring the grand-children home to visit. They soothe my pain, lessen my burdens, and bring me joy.

My last child was my son, Christopher. He is a wonderful boy and, like his sisters before him, he seems to be more intelligent and compassionate than the average 11-year-old boy. At his young age, he's already braved a great many battles in his life–some of which have left permanent scars. At the age of eight, he had his front tooth knocked out on the playground at school. Last year, he had his arm broken, again on the playground. The 'book learning' comes easily for him, but the social aspects of school have made his life difficult–at times even unbearable. Unlike my daughters, he has trouble making friends. He recently 'graduated' from the sixth grade at Holy Cross Catholic School in Lena and has never been invited to a single birthday party, even though there are kids who attend his every year. I'm grateful they show up, if for no other reason than it's hard to have a party if there's no one there.

If this all sounds a little sad, I guess it is; but I'm telling you these things only to set the stage for something wonderful that happened at his graduation mass. After a long and touching ceremony, the 'graduates' passed out flowers to their parents. As the class was small and lined up alphabetically, my son (with a last name being with 'C') was the first child in line. He gave me my flower in front of the alter, and then the principal of the school informed the congregation that my son had a few words he wished to say to the crowd. I was stunned. I gave him a hug and returned to my spot in the pew, uncertain and nervous of what was about to take place.

Although he's almost as big as me, he looked so small standing behind the lectern, gazing out at the congregation with eyes as large as saucers. Then the boy who was so shy and uncertain, so afraid of what others might think of him, stood before a church full of people and began to speak. He said he wanted to share a few things about his experience at the school that the students were all about to leave. Remembering his pain throughout the years, and the way he had been shunned, I braced myself and thought, 'Here it comes.'

And he did talk about the school, and he told the truth about no one really liking him too well, but he made light of it. He even had the congregation laughing at one point. He said that, as time went on, kids picked on him less–he speculated that they must have gotten bored with the whole deal. He found no blame, pointed no fingers, and looked for no sympathy. He thanked the school and everyone who had gotten him this far; he even disclosed how he had tried going to a different school in hope that things would be better, but that he had come back to Holy Cross because he'd missed the kids, the teachers, Father, and the church.

I was stunned. This boy, my child of eleven years, had taken his heartache and turned it into something positive. He had, in his own unique way, won at a game that I'd long ago given up on as being hopeless. In those few moments, as he spoke, I saw a glimpse of the man he would one day become. And my heart became lighter, because I knew now–for the first time–that he was going to be okay. Really okay.

So today, I am selfishly writing my weekly article for my son. I know not what lies ahead, but I wanted to thank him for showing me how much class and true grit he's managed to scrape together. He has taught me the meaning of compassion, survival, and the true measure of self-worth–all this from an eleven year old boy. I don't know if the middle school that he'll be attending in fall is ready for him. For eleven years, *I've* been struggling to be 'ready', but he has always seemed to stay at least one step ahead of me.

So spread your wings, my son, in practice flight. Though you are not yet ready to leave the nest, I know I've already seen your shadow passing over as you soar above me. Still, may the winds that bring your fortune never carry you too far from home.

A Need for Discipline

No matter what opinions you may hold regarding raising children, I am sure you could find documented studies, or entire books that were written, claiming that *your* views are correct. Some experts say children should never be spanked. They claim that spanking is a violent act, and thereby teaches children that violence is an acceptable means of dealing with people–even people who are smaller and weaker than you. Other experts say that children should be taught by positive reinforcement. Reward good behavior and ultimately the child will learn to be good. Some say that 'time-outs' are a useful tool. Others believe taking favorite games or other privileges away can correct a child's unacceptable behavior.

It's hard to say which experts are right. To further complicate things, no two children are alike. A method of discipline that works extremely well on one child may not work on his/her siblings at all. I've often said that each child should come with an individual instruction manual; but such books would probably weigh as much as the child, and would certainly complicate the entire birthing process. Having a baby is painful enough without adding the discomfort of paper cuts to the list.

But children are our future and, to be honest, that frightens me. They seem to be running wild as of late . . . although I suppose every generation has made that same claim. Still, it seems to ring very true, and I've been trying to understand 'why'. Maybe with more and more kids being raised in a two-income home (or a single parent home), parents are more apt to give their children whatever they desire, at whatever the price. It's easier to buy the latest video game than it is to find several hours of quality time to spend with a child. I've fallen into this trap many times myself. We feel guilty because we're away so much, so we try to compensate by offering gifts–trinkets–which prove that we love them. But, it can be argued that discipline is a gift as well.

We've all been there–in a checkout line with the young mother who's trying her best to control two kids afoot and prop up a third one in the cart. One child is screaming because the other one punched him, and the other is screaming because, no matter what toy he holds up and begs his mother to buy (and he's tried them all, one by one), she says 'no' and quietly asks him to put it back. The young boy finally throws himself against the cart and shouts to the entire store (and half a city block) that he hates her and is going to run away. My gut instinct at that moment is, '*Please do!*' But I ultimately find myself asking, 'What has led to the behavior, and what could the young mother possibly do at that point to stop it?' Granted, a public place is the worst setting to begin a discipline program, yet I firmly believe that something has to be done.

Discipline begins at home, and should be done with love–not anger. I saw a bumper sticker yesterday that read, "America needs parent control–not gun control." My gratitude and admiration go out to the people who spend their lives working with, and trying to discipline, our children–not only because they deal with children like the ones described above, but also because they have to deal with us, the parents. Say what you want; things are not like they used to be. When I was in school, or just riding the bus, I knew better than to break the rules. If I did and my parents were notified, it would have been a very unpleasant situation, to say the least. Now, when teachers and bus drivers try to control children, parents still get angry, but the anger seems to be aimed at the teachers and drivers, not at the child who committed the infraction–or at themselves, for failing the child on a very basic level.

We, as a society, have managed to successfully tie the hands of those who have chosen to lead our children into the future. Our own lack of respect–for ourselves, our children, and those with whom we share this world–has led to our children's lack of respect for authority of any kind.

As with all observations, this one isn't universal. It doesn't apply to all children. There are still a large number of 'good' kids out there, but the bad ones are making life tough for them–and ultimately for us as well. We, as a society, aren't doing ourselves any favors by being so tolerant of that which is unacceptable. Discipline and respect are forever connected, and our children need to learn of both.

Fathers

They come into the world, very much the same . . . little boys who cling to their mothers and admire their fathers. Time passes, and too quickly, the world turns. The boys become young men, squaring off against the world. They view themselves as strong, sure, and indestructible. They question all the laws, bend all the rules, and believe they will live forever.

As fate would have it, the young man falls in love. He survives the courtship and somehow muddles through the wedding ceremony, complete with all the trimmings. Though he may now be more 'settled', he is much unchanged. Then, one day it happens. The nurse places his first-born child in his arms, and the world changes. He is a father now, and nothing will ever be the same. He looks down and sees this new person–this tiny, little life–who now depends on him for everything. Suddenly, he has a family to consider and all of his decisions, for the rest of his life, weigh heavier and carry more clout. Gone is the feeling of careless freedom–weightless and fleeting. All of that is over. He is a father now.

And the truth of the matter is, the children he raises will not be aware of the sacrifices he makes, not until they are grown and have children of their own. They will not know of the heavy responsibility that he shoulders–the decisions and choices he makes, the opportunities he turns down–always with his family foremost in mind. Like an invisible weight, that responsibility is always present. He shifts the load, carrying it so lightly that even he seems to forget that it's there. He doesn't mind the burden, or any price that he must pay. He is a father.

And one day, many years into the journey, he will watch as his own sons break away. And he will anticipate the trials that await them and the mistakes that they will claim, because they were once his trials and his mistakes . . . many, many years before. And he'll walk his daughters down the aisle and give them away–to other young men who have yet to face the test. Swollen with pride, he holds back his tears. He is strong to the end; he is a father.

In younger days, he carried his children in steady arms, familiar and secure. His eyes often twinkled and his laughter was hard-won. His voice could be gentle, or thunder like a storm. His words were the law–still are, to this day. He is a father. And if he remembers all of the dreams he set aside, he never mentions them. And if asked what being a father had cost him over the years, he will shrug and dismiss the topic. He knows, as only a father can, that he's been well paid–paid with tiny smiles, wilted bouquets of flowering weeds, and light, airy kisses given by a child. He feels compensated by the knowledge that they are his children. He gave them life, raised them up, and gave them independence. And then he stepped aside, but not too far. He is a father.

To Mothers Everywhere

This coming Sunday we will celebrate Mothers' Day–one day of an entire year set aside to acknowledge and remember the strongest and most giving member of our families. She is the one who sits up with a sick child far into the night, or is awakened from a sound sleep by a child's voice calling out in the stillness, "Mom, I threw up!" She is the one who ties the shoes, packs the lunches, washes and folds the clothes, and kisses skinned knees to make them all better. She is a chameleon–easily shifting from one role to another; she is a mentor, friend, role model, disciplinarian, adventurer, teacher, cook, maid, wife, and lover. She is a woman in the very best sense of the word–strong enough to give guidance and gentle enough to mend a child's broken dreams.

She is tired, overworked, and often underappreciated. Like all of the greatest blessings in our lives, we notice her most when she isn't there. She loves us for who we are (even though she doesn't always understand what that is), and she loves us enough to step aside and allow us to make our own mistakes. A mother never says, "You deserved it" when something *bad* happens–only something good. And a mother never says, "I told you so," when the pain of our failure has already been punishment enough. A mother always leaves a light on for her children–even if they're grown and gone. Her heart, and her door, are always open.

A mother is a beacon in a cold and endless night. She is a strong arm we can hold onto and a familiar lap in which we can rest. The world may change, and dreams may crash and shatter, but a mother's love is eternal–from one generation to the next. She molds the world and shapes young souls. No job is more fulfilling, or more tiring. It offers no paid holidays and no overtime compensation. A mother never 'punches out', and never leaves the position unattended. It is the most consuming and demanding position a woman can accept, and also the most rewarding. Anyone who doubts that has never bathed in the love of a child's smile. May the upcoming holiday be a special day for all mothers; heaven knows they deserve it.

Overlooked Treasures

I think we should start a new holiday. We could call it 'Overlooked Treasures Day', and we would use it to celebrate our children. That might sound a little crazy–setting aside a day to honor the little people in our lives who track mud across the clean floor, draw pictures on the bathroom mirror with toothpaste, and who desperately need to use a restroom ten minutes into a long car ride. Let's face it; these little creations–our daughters and sons–are as unique as they are entertaining. They can lock a sibling in the closet, but can't pour cereal into a bowl without spilling it. They can work the remote for the television, stereo, and garage door–but can't remember to raise the toilet seat (or put it down, depending on the circumstances). They can even create amazing works of art using nothing more than a box of Crayola crayons . . . which is part of the problem. They often seem to forget that their masterpieces belong on paper, not on the bedroom wall. But still, I propose a holiday.

I have three grandsons who know me as being a bit crazy, at least for a grandmother. This means that I'm all for wrestling them down on the living room carpet and chewing on their belly if that's what it takes to get them to giggle and squeal. There's not much for cookies at my house, but I'll chase them around the table if they dare me. Of course, as they get older (and faster), my odds of catching them will start to decline–but it will still be worth a try.

And yet, despite the horseplay and the closeness that we share, they are not mine, not in the same way that their mother was mine. They are hers, and that makes it a little different. My own youngest child is twelve now, so my days of Crayola drawings and evenings spent telling stories with my child settled in my lap are gone. With a touch of nostalgia, I watch the world around me. I hear the young mothers lose their patience in stores and scold their little ones a bit too loudly. I see the children with the soiled clothes and unkempt hair. I see children with sad eyes following busy parents, like invisible shadows who are only meant to tag along. More and more, it seems that we grownups are losing track of the important things in life. We're losing track of the children.

My proposed 'Overlooked Treasures Day' would not be for giving gifts or eating candy. We would not celebrate it with gaily-wrapped packages. The only thing we would share on that day would be ourselves. We have forgotten that children are magical. They can make you laugh and cry in the same minute. A child can break your heart with a single tear, or mend your soul with one small hug. They are our greatest commodity, and the most precious of all gifts that life will bring our way. They are unique and irreplaceable, and they are ours forever; we are bound at the heart. Our children deserve our time, our love, and our respect. They need to be held fast and nurtured while they are small, or they will never soar when they are older. And, if they don't soar, let it not be because we failed them. In fact, everyday should be an 'Overlooked Treasures Day', because that's what our children deserve. No less. After all, they will never know how special they are if even their parents forget to tell them.

Only on Loan

You're never quite sure what a child is going to say. Their innocence, coupled with their lack of inhibition, makes them pipe up in grocery stores everywhere with questions like, "Why is that woman so fat?" or "Mommy, I really have to *go!*" Sometimes their spontaneity is charming, sometimes not. But one thing is for sure, when a child talks, someone ought to be listening.

My children are all older now. My son, the youngest, is 14. He's caught in that awkward age between childhood and being all grown up. He's like a six-month-old puppy whose paws are still too big. He's going from cute and cuddly to mature and handsome–and he's not at all certain he even wants to make the trip. When you're a puppy, you can get away with a lot more stuff. He's wise enough to know that.

In spite of his youth, he and I have made a habit of engaging in deep and meaningful conversations. He is, and always has been, wise beyond his years. We discuss profound things. We talk about what motivates people to do what they do. This topic is especially popular when it's time for him to do his chores. As the teenage years claim him, the road seems to be getting a little rockier. His answers to my questions are quicker and more abrupt–like there are a million things he'd rather be doing than talking to Mom. For the most part, I take it in stride. There were days, not long ago, when we talked about abstract concepts–like old souls and the meaning of life. Having had those talks, I know in my heart that there are strong and steadfast beliefs buried within my stubborn, teenage son's head, and that's a good thing.

I had a hectic schedule last week. It was a string of days when I'd race from one thing to another and yet nothing really seemed to get done. Unable to find it elsewhere in my life, I gambled and turned to my son for validation. That's dangerous to do with a teenager; there's no telling what they might say.

We were riding in the car at the time, which is now one of the few places I can still corner him for a talk. When we're home, he's in his room and the door is closed. He's bonding with the computer. I've discovered that, if I open the door to initiate a conversation, I'm usually greeted with, "What do you want?" My answer is definitely *not* another puppy.

So there we were, driving along, and in my moment of weakness, I asked my son, "If I were gone tomorrow, what would you remember best about me?" Is that going out on a limb or what? His reaction, like most of what he does as of late, was not what I expected. I was prepared for an answer like, "I don't know" or "What kind of a stupid question is that?" Instead he immediately started laughing. When I could pry out of him what it was he found so amusing, he said–between giggles–that "I gave him food". That was it. No profound wisdom, no golden nugget I could cling to in my spreading moment of weakness. I was merely a walking, talking distributor of hamburgers and frozen TV dinners. Having heard that, I was suddenly reminded of a lesson I already knew; validation can be hard to come by.

And yet, his answer was perfect. You see, someday (soon I hope), he will be able to get his own food. Literally. At that point, he'll be one step closer to slipping away. Is there pain in that realization? More than I could ever say. But I know that my children are not really mine. They are on loan to me, for a very short while, during which time it is my job to prepare them for the day when they will leave. They are not mine to keep. They are mine to love, and nurture, then watch fly away. Hopefully, God willing, they'll make it just fine out in that great, big world–and that, I believe, is my validation.

Raising Children

If you have children, you've spent a large part of your adult life being responsible for another human being. In fact, when your first child was born, it changed your life forever. In those early weeks and months, you might have thought that the worst part was the fussy period the infant may have gone through on a daily basis–perhaps crying incessantly regardless of what you tried to do. Or maybe the biggest challenge to get through was the midnight feedings; once that baby slept all night, you'd have it made. Or so you thought. But those, my friends, were the easy problems.

I don't care how many children you have–every one is different. For some reason, the firstborn is often good-natured and easy-going. It sleeps all night at an early age and listens when you tell him/her 'no'. This child wouldn't dream of grabbing all the lamp cords and pulling the lamps onto the floor the minute you turn your back. (How dare you indulge yourself with a trip into the bathroom; children must be watched!) The firstborn will allow you to do that from time to time, and will leave the house standing pretty much the same way you left it.

There's a reason for this. The first child is easy-going so that you're tricked into having more. After all, the little angel will need someone to play with. Enter child number two.

The secondborn child comes into the world on a mission; it must make sure you experience all the things you missed out on with child number one. Oh, it will sleep for twelve hours straight, but only during the day. Once past the crawling stage, this child will climb with the courage and determination of a mountain goat. Whether hungry or not, it will attempt to eat items that were never meant to be consumed by any human, let alone an infant–treats such as coffee grounds from the garbage, dirt from the entryway floor, cat and/or dog food, and potting soil complete with plants. You would think that, after having such a child, there would never be a third. But parents are survivors–and they're too damn tired by this point to care. The house is already under siege. It's too late for damage control, so bring 'em on!

Ultimately, 'having' children means 'raising' children, but how do we do that? How do we take tiny individuals and turn them into rational, productive, happy human beings? Only by the grace of God, I guess. At times, it's hard–very hard. When you know what your child is capable of doing, but they refuse to try; when they're hurting because they don't feel like they fit in; when they struggle through the same mistakes you yourself made, even though you warned them–time and again. I'll take the midnight feedings over those problems any day. It helps, if only a little, to remind yourself that it's all temporary. Eventually, they'll muddle through and find their way. Eventually, they'll leave, taking your heart with them. But that was the plan all along, wasn't it? You have to love them enough to let them go.

And after all the struggles–years later when the quiet once again settles over your house–you'll stumble upon little memories, tucked safely away in that quiet spot in your mind. Those recollections are payment in full for the time you spent. For me, such memories include my second-grade daughter coming home in tears because her teacher wanted her to bring in some 'knee wax' for cleaning her desk and she didn't know what it was. After some discussion, I discovered the mystery item was 'elbow grease', and she supplied plenty. There are the memories of how she and her sister would fight, but beware to anyone who tried to come between them–or hurt one or the other. They were inseparable, those two, and as different as night and day. I'm proud to say they still are.

And, of course, I have the memory of my son's kindergarten screening. I walked him in, feeling proud as a peacock. After all, wasn't he already beginning to read? Didn't he know all his colors and love to do puzzles? Still, by the time we left, I was sure they had listed him as a 'special needs' child. The questions they asked at the screening were simple enough. "Where are your ears?" and "Where is your nose?" They asked him to count, and identify his colors and letters. For the most part, my son was unresponsive. They even tossed him a ball to check his reflexes. He allowed it to hit him in the middle of his chest and never even tried to catch it. I was stunned. We left the school as we had arrived, hand-in-hand, but strangely quiet.

"Why wouldn't you answer their questions; why wouldn't you tell them what they wanted to know?" I asked softly when I couldn't stand the silence any longer.

"Well," he informed me, "I never heard so many stupid questions in all my life. If they don't know where my ears are, *I'm* not going to tell them!"

I'd done it again, stumbled upon one of those rare moments when my child's simple logic had rendered me powerless and in awe.

Children. Love them, cherish them, and let them go. They'll come back, time and again–sometimes in need, sometimes just to touch base. They are your only claim to eternity, and more than just a blessing for today.

Part 3: Seasonal

A January Night

January, the dead of winter. I lie awake at night and listen to the wind outside my window. It sounds cold and lonely, on its way to somewhere it doesn't care to go. It is not the same wind that I hear on a summer night–the one that plays with careless abandon, whispering through leaves on its way to greet a gentle dawn. The wind on a January night travels alone, snapping at the heels of the darkness like a starving dog, its teeth sharp and quick.

There is the faint sound of scratching in the night. The naked branches of bushes rub up against the house, begging to be let in, where they might find some warmth. Caught in dreamless slumber, they've forgotten the departed summer and crickets chirping from beneath the deck. I pull my covers up over my head, hoping to escape the lonely sound of their frozen, windswept dance, but the wind has caught them up in her embrace, and the song they move to plays long into the night.

Here, in the dead of winter, lies the very secret of a man's soul. In this time of stillness and solitude, when the sun teases the sky but will not share her warm embrace, one finds the meaning of faith. Now, when the nights are long and the days short, there is more to believe in than the simple miracle of spring. If life can be born, time and again, from the frozen land, who can begin to say what the human heart is capable of delivering? We are far more than a winter wind lost in the darkness. When we cry out through the frozen air, we should take heed to listen for an answer. Unlike the wind, we do not travel alone. The Son is there, we need only believe.

A Thought for the New Year

Another holiday season, and another year, have come and gone. Although my Christmas tree will still be up for another week or two, and the outside lights will continue to add their touch of color to the cold, frosty nights, I am not reflecting on a holiday season just past; I am looking ahead to the brand new year.

What will it bring? What surprises await us in the months ahead–what will Lady Luck choose to send our way? To be honest, I'm not sure I believe in 'luck', either good or bad. I think sometimes things just happen. Sometimes, we spend a dollar on a lottery ticket and discover it's a winner. On another day, we might spend $2500 on a car that dies 300 miles later–with no guarantee. Good luck? Bad luck? Not necessarily. Things just happen, and we find ourselves on the receiving end. I guess that's life; the important thing is how we deal with it and all of its little surprises.

Think about it. If we believe in luck, then we have to justify it. If you have a string of good luck, you might start believing you did something to earn it. The same thing can be said for bad luck. It's far too easy to be negative and sad when we feel that luck is working against us. Eliminate luck, and what do you have? You have yourself, your life . . . and perhaps a smidgen of fate.

Some will argue that fate is the same thing as luck, but I'd disagree. Luck tends to come and go, with no real purpose and no real value. Fate, if you believe in it, is the power that draws us toward what we're supposed to be. Both fate and luck can be cruel or kind. Luck does it for her own amusement; fate does it to prod us along in the direction we are meant to take. Fate is like a large, warm, familiar hand–guiding us, steering us, perhaps even carrying us when we grow too weary. Luck is a shot in the dark–a loud noise, a clap, then it's gone. Luck is a traveling companion, gilded by fear and uncertainty; while fate is a tool, used by a Father.

Whether you believe in luck or fate, I hope your New Year is a good one. I hope your blessings are many and your heartaches few. I hope you find time to count the blessings you already have, and more time to seek those you hope to achieve. I wish you love, and peace, and a sense of purpose. And, if you're still a firm believer in Lady Luck, I hope she's riding on your shoulder all the way. May fate be gentle as you find your way through the months ahead, and may your faith, in a higher power and/or yourself, be strong. As each new year unfolds, it is a trip filled with wonder, and there are surprises at every turn. Make the most of this one . . . hold fast to your faith, and let the journey begin!

Happy New Year

I've heard it said that the secret to a good life lies in keeping everything in balance. So much work, then so much play; a sufficient amount of food, then enough activity to work it off; a set number of sunny days for each one with rain; so many smiles for each and every frown. Everything in moderation, that's the key.

It's an easy concept to embrace when we're in the middle of the sunny days, friends are all around us, and we can still squeeze into our tight pair of jeans. (That last one might be for women only!) We forget all about moderation when we're getting what we want, and we're liking it! But let the clouds move in and we pout like children. Suddenly, we're convinced that life isn't fair and the cards are stacked against us. We definitely don't like 'balance' when we're sitting on the 'bad' side of the scale.

Well, seeing that it's a brand new year, let's break the rules. At least for a day or two, let's pretend that the 'experts' are wrong. Let's believe that there's no such thing as 'balance'. With that in mind, here are a few of my New Year Wishes for you:

- May you never run out of hot water while you're still in the shower.

- May the price of gas go up only *after* you've filled your tank.

- May the 'fat-free' version of anything you buy taste just as good as its evil counterpart.

- May your income tax refund be larger than you expected, and may your property taxes go down (remember, we're dreaming here, so we might as well dream big!)

- May you be happy, healthy, and surrounded by love.

- May your cherished pet–your friend and constant companion–live to be a ripe, old age, then die peacefully in its sleep on a soft, summer's eve.

- May you be employed in a job you truly love, one that you can take pride in.

- May they never make your favorite brand of laundry detergent "new and improved".

- May you never give anyone else the power to make you feel foolish.

- May your checkbook always balance.

- And finally, may you believe in one dream–any dream–enough to be willing to work at making it come true.

Chocolate-Chip Cookies and Willpower

What is it about one year ending and another beginning that fills us with such excitement–or despair? Is it the hope that the new year will bring us closer to our dreams, or the fear that nothing will change? How many New Year's resolutions are made (and ultimately broken), until we finally don't bother to make them anymore? For some reason we think that, because it's a new year, we will find the strength and the willpower to change what we don't like about ourselves. We'll lose weight, stop smoking, be nicer to our friends (and more tolerant of our enemies), spend more time with the family, keep a cleaner house, work harder, save more money, or finish that scrapbook that we started years ago. But, as January fades into February, we are forced to admit that we are no different than we were way back in December–or even the December before that.

There's nothing magical about changing, just as there's nothing magical about making a New Year's resolution. If you want your life to be different–if you really want to change–you need only know 'how' to make it happen. Here's a fact that may surprise you–change does not require willpower. In fact, willpower is nothing more than a label we give to the act of consciously making different choices in our lives; and, it is in our choices that change resides. We are, for all our wisdom and glory, nothing more than creatures of habit. We do what we do when we do it because, in some way, it's working for us.

For example, I'll share something with you about myself that I really hate. I eat when I'm frustrated. When there are issues I'd rather not face, or I have problems I can't resolve, I dive into the cookie jar. It's never been scientifically proven, but I am certain that it's quite impossible to worry and nibble on a chocolate-chip cookie at the same time. The reason that turning to a chocolate-chip cookie for comfort is a bad thing is that any and all problems have a much longer lifespan than a cookie does. So, one cookie becomes two, then three or four. Before you know it, you have another problem. The cookie jar is empty and nothing has been resolved.

So ask yourself, do you really want to change? If the answer is 'yes', then make only one resolution, and don't do it exclusively on December 31st. Do it as often as you must. Do it over and over until you get it right. Here's the resolution: resolve to be honest with yourself. That's it. Take the time to listen if your heart is crying, instead of silencing it with cookies. Take the time to ask yourself the questions you've been avoiding. "Is this what life is about?" or "Am I happy, and if not–why not?" "If I could be anything or anyone at all, what or who would I be?" Then, after asking, sit quietly and listen for the answer. Be patient. You'd do as much for a friend, so do it for yourself.

Each of us has one life to live. No more, no less. If you're not living yours to the fullest, ask yourself, "Why not?" No one can hold you back but you. So resolve to be honest. Compassionately listen to the voice inside of you–it speaks only to you; so, if you don't listen, no one will. Do it today. Don't wait for that surge of willpower. It doesn't exist. I believed in willpower once. I even thought that I had it, but I was wrong. It was only a temporary sugar-rush from all of those cookies.

They're Here!

The gardening catalogs have arrived; can spring be far behind? Even with this year's lack of snow, winter has still held us hostage. Every year is the same; I enjoy winter for the break it gives from mowing the lawn and weeding the flower beds, but the arrival of the seed catalogs always makes me wish that I was once again outside, puttering around in the dirt.

I order plants every spring. When you've got several acres to work with, as I do, there's plenty of room for trying new things. Before long, through the application of trial and error, you begin to get a good idea of what will grow for you and what won't. I've tried growing 'butterfly bushes' several times (without any luck), but I have yucca plants and goblin blanket flowers that are threatening to take over the yard. They are both plants that thrive on neglect–which probably explains why they do so well for me.

I don't have much of a 'traditional' garden. By that, I mean that I don't have carrots, and peas, and sweet corn all growing in nice, neat rows the way my mother does. I used to do that sort of thing–years ago–but I've given up on it. For one thing, my son doesn't eat home-grown vegetables. He would die if you forced him to eat lettuce, and he thinks that tomatoes are gross. He does like carrots and sweet corn, but unfortunately so do all of the deer in the area. As they seem to spend more time harvesting items out of the garden than we do (and at a much earlier date), I've given up on that battle.

My garden consists of rows of raspberry canes, a few tomato and cucumber plants for me to enjoy, and a lot of flowers–which have no nutritional value, but make me smile every time I look out the window and see them. A short distance from the flowers is a row of Nanking cherry bushes, which give me more cherries than I know what to do with. Their fruit is small, but it works well for making jelly and syrup. I often freeze some cherries and some extra raspberries, then cook them up into sauce in the dead of winter. The smell of fruit simmering on the stove forces the winter doldrums away.

So, I study each and every gardening catalog as it arrives. Every few days, there's yet another one waiting in my mailbox when I get home from work. It's fun to order something new and unfamiliar, but beware. The experienced gardener knows that his plants will probably never look as good as the pictures in the catalog. In fact, you're lucky if they even survive.

I often wonder how many millions of plants get shipped out of nurseries each spring, and how many of those actually make it once they're planted in their new homes. I'll bet more die than survive, but that's the trouble with being a flower or tree–you're stuck trying to grow wherever you're planted. People don't have it quite so bad, yet many times I'll bet that we don't reach our full potential, either. Instead of growing and thriving, we waste too much time envying others for their better fortune–their bigger cars, nicer homes, better jobs. Let's face it–not everyone can be a rose. And is that so bad? Think about it, with all of the strikes it has against it, notice how the dandelion still thrives and multiplies.

So, glean some wisdom from the pictures that decorate the annual seed catalogs. Notice how, by being different, each plant and flower has its own unique role to fill and a different place to thrive in. Grow into whatever you're meant to be–whether it's a petunia or a cabbage plant. I'd hate to think that the Master Gardener will look down someday and be disappointed that you didn't bloom where you were planted.

Chocolate, Cards, Roses and Guilt

Happy Valentine's Day! Once again, we are presented with yet another occasion on which to buy gifts, give flowers, and try to show someone how special he or she is in our lives. In many ways, this day is yet another reason for stores to decorate their windows and entice us to spend our hard-earned money in an attempt to 'stay out of the doghouse', or remain in someone's good graces. Wow, that sounds pretty cynical, but I guess I'm just February's version of Scrooge.

Still, in my own defense, aside from breaking up the cold, dreary month of February–what use is it? Do we really need an excuse to buy someone a card; and aren't chocolates for sale throughout the year? Let's be honest, if you really love someone, you'd better show it every day–not just on February 14th!

And let's not forget the guilt factor that's built into this holiday. Why is it that the hopeless romantic is often coupled with a forgetful partner? One buys a card; the other forgets. One finds the perfect gift; the other decides it's not worth the hassle. Or, worse yet, neither can afford to buy that special gift–the one that says how they truly feel. Being broke, and in love, seems hardest on Valentine's Day.

In an attempt to understand the tradition of this day, I did a little research on it. Very little. What I learned is that, in ancient Rome, they had a festival of Lupercalia, which was celebrated on Feb. 15th. It was a day set aside to honor the Roman gods Juno and Pan. Some part of that ancient ritual revolved around procreation and fertility rites. Now, there's a motive for buying cards and candy!

My research also taught me that there were two saints in 3rd century Rome who both went by the name of Valentine. Their feast day is jointly celebrated on February 14th, but the holiday (as we know it today) has no apparent connection to either man. In fact, according to my Compton Encyclopedia, our tradition of celebrating Valentine's Day probably started in England and France sometime around the fourteenth century. In those days, young people would celebrate the evening of the 14th by gathering and placing their names in a box. You then became the valentine of the person whose name was paired with yours through a random drawing. I will concede that such an outing would be a nice social event with which to fill a winter's night, but it's hardly the making of a tradition that went on to endure for more than six hundred years.

Yet, here we are. I suppose, with Easter a whole two months away, we would be wise to enjoy whatever diversions come our way. So, if Valentine's Day is a big deal in your book, I hope you receive a wonderful, romantic card and a box of only the finest chocolate. If you're young (or old) and in love for the first (or last) time, the day may well hold some magic. But for the veteran couples who have been down this road countless times, the security of each other's company means more than any card or gift, bought at any price. So, make the most of this day, and every day to follow. Maybe, just to be different, take the money you would have spent on a gift or a card and donate it to our local animal shelter, or a food pantry for the needy. It can easily be argued that Valentine's Day, like every other holiday, is exactly what you make of it. For me, it's just another day–with one exception. There has always been a mystery that surrounds this holiday. How can it be possible to gain *five* pounds from eating a one-pound box of chocolate?

Here Comes the Tax Return!

In the spirit of the season, I've been trying to decide what to do with my tax return check. My first impulse, not only this year but every year, is to race out and spend it. After all, consumer spending is supposed to strengthen the economy, and I should at least try to do my share. Yet, when it comes right down to it, I can't think of anything that I really need. Oh, there are some things that I *want*, but that's not quite the same thing.

For example, at one point in time I was going to buy a dishwasher with one of my tax returns. It sounded simple (and tempting) enough, but my cupboards are arranged in such a way that I would have had to order an apartment-size unit, to the tune of nearly $400. Besides, let's be honest here, for the amount of cooking I do I could wash the dishes by hand for a long, long time before I could truly justify spending that kind of money. And, with my mother living next door, I could give up cooking and baking altogether and I'd still be pleasingly plump. For these reasons, I never did buy the dishwasher.

I've also toyed with the thought of putting a three-season room on the front of my house. That would be great, if for no other reason than I'd no longer have a patio door that opens up to nothing but a four-foot drop to the ground below. After nine years living in this house, I don't think that's too much to want. To do that, though, I'd need a building permit, some lumber, a good plan, and lots of hard work. The worst part, though, is that my property taxes would go up. This type of thinking tends to take the fun out of everything! Needless to say, my patio door remains patio-less.

So, back to spending my tax return. I don't need any furniture. Being an upholsterer, it seems I've collected enough chairs and couches to last a lifetime. I suppose I could order some new fabric–some *nice* fabric–and redo a few of my pieces. The couch I upholstered ten years ago is due for another covering, and I've got a turn-of-the-century couch in my basement that is screaming for a beautiful tapestry or brocade. But do I want to go through all of that trouble just so my cats can shed on a different-colored fabric? I'll have to think about that for a while.

I don't need another vehicle (not that my return is ever *that* big!). At 69,000 miles, I'm first getting my current car broken in. Besides, I drive a little Ford Aspire and I keep hoping that, if I hang onto it long enough, I'll get to see what it will be when it 'grows up.' I could buy some more restoration parts for my '66 truck, but I figure it's going to be a few years before I get that project done–especially at the rate that I've been working on it. So, let's do the math . . . My son is currently 13 ½ years old. Hmmm–a restored pickup truck and a teenage driver residing at the same address. Maybe I'll hold off on ordering those parts a little while longer.

I know what I can do–I'll get myself a new bed! I sleep in a twin bed now; a simple metal-frame structure that holds up a 5-inch mattress on a network of interlocking springs. It's actually the bottom half of a bunk bed I received as payment for some upholstery work I did. But, to be honest, it's just about the most comfortable thing I've ever slept on. I sink into its center and the covers close in around me. I absolutely love it! Besides, it's just the right size for me and one cat. What more could I want at the end of a long day? (That I could buy with my tax return, that is!)

Happy Easter

Okay, just for the record, I don't color Easter eggs. The thought of watching over several small bowls of colored liquid, waiting for the eggs to be "dark" enough, sounds about as thrilling to me as watching paint dry. Let's face it, they're only going to be smashed into little pieces and eaten, or tossed out because everyone is sick of looking at them after several days. Oh sure, the kids have fun searching for them after that energetic, old rabbit hides them all over the house, but we all know how that *really* turns out:

"Mommy, he stole my eggs!"

"Did not, I found them all fair and square!"

"You stole them and I'm telling!"

Or (and this is always a good one):

"Mommy, Mommy, look at all the eggs we found!"

Mother counts the eggs and discovers that they haven't found at least four of the dyed creations–but which four? She peers into the future and is met by horrific visions of rotten, boiled eggs awaiting discovery by some hapless victim. She replies, a painted smile on her face, "You'd better go look some more, you might not have them all."

"Sure we do, Mommy. We got them all, see?"

The child raises the basket containing several eggs and assorted pieces of Easter candy for her mother to review. Mother now has a dilemma. To argue with the child would mean that she has inside knowledge of how many eggs were actually hidden. This would also suggest an inside connection between herself and the rabbit–and she really doesn't want to go there. The child breaks the reverie by announcing, "We're tired of looking. We're going to go and eat our candy now."

The kids disappear to begin the chocolate, hyper-active phase of the holiday while mother stares warily around the house–wondering where the missing eggs could be. She recalls that fateful year when the foolish bunny had hidden an egg in someone's boot, which–due to lack of rain or snow–went unworn for a long period of time. One rainy July afternoon, a scream had come from the entryway and a child, hopping on one foot, had appeared in the kitchen–the remnants of a crushed egg clinging to her sock. It had not been a pretty sight.

Also, just for the record, I only 'allowed' the Easter Bunny to hide those baskets of future cavities and inconvenient dental appointments around my house because I knew the kids wanted to look for them. Besides, a basket brimming with Hershey's chocolate that goes undetected is a lot less threatening than boiled, organic, time bombs. And, in all honesty, if I'm hiding *chocolate* in the house, I'm certainly not about to forget where I hid it–I'm not *that* stupid. If the kids don't find it within the hour, it's all mine!

It's not that I have anything against Easter, I really don't. I tend to treat all holidays with an equal amount of neglect and denial. I don't hang red hearts (or any variation thereof) around my house in February–or green shamrocks in March; I don't light off fireworks in July, and I definitely don't scrape sticky, orange pulp out of pumpkins in October, then attack them with a sharp object to create scary faces. And, as far as the traditional Thanksgiving turkey goes, I make turkey several times during the year. Why should the one that finds its way into my oven in November be deemed more special? Even at Easter, I am tempted to say, "Bah, humbug!" but I'd either be several months early or late–I'll let you decide which.

I suppose that, if I had a lot of money, I could schedule a whole mess of counseling sessions that would tell me why I am the way I am. And it's not just holidays that get to me. I also hate parades. I cry like a baby at every one, so I suppose it's easy to understand why I want to avoid them. As fate would have it, the house I now live in is located right on the annual parade route. The entire procession marches right past my front porch. God does, indeed, have a sense of humor!

I rationalize the whole anti-holiday thing by explaining that everything is just too commercialized. Everything seems to be centered around spending money–whether it's decorating, or feeding the extended family a five-course meal, or just giving gifts. My mother recently told me that she's waiting for a good sale so that she can buy her Easter ham. She hasn't found one yet, but I've no doubt she'll keep on searching. She loves this sort of thing, and I suppose that–in a way–I envy her for that. It just seems that everyone is getting busier and busier, so we use the holidays as excuses to get together and say how much we care. When you think about it, it's more than a little sad. We really shouldn't need an excuse.

Looking to Easter

Easter is early this year. Colored eggs and baskets of candy, stuffed bunnies and white lilies are everywhere. I note these things even as I confess–I am still not a holiday person. I find it hard to get caught up in the excitement of an egg hunt, or thrilled at the thought of sitting down to an Easter ham. Holidays are incapable of generating love. They only offer an opportunity to share it. We have that opportunity every day. We just don't seem to see it.

I don't fully understand why society sets aside certain days of the year to remember what's really important. When it's Christmas time, I must admit I get caught up in the feeling of generosity and goodwill that seems to be so prevalent. The 'magic' of the season is the love and joy that people bring to it–but why just at Christmas; why not the whole year? Now it's Easter, and we are reminded that an ultimate sacrifice was made for us. Someone loved us enough to give up His life–and trusted His Father enough to carry Him home. Yes, remind us. But eventually I pray that we won't have to be reminded. It's not just an 'Easter' gift, but one for each and every day.

Spring

According to the calendar at least, it's my favorite time of year. You may favor the bustle of the holidays, or the long, lazy days of summer, but for me spring is the very best season of all.

It has not arrived quickly this year, but seemed instead to tease us with its indifferent approach. I can remember years when winter was gone in an instant. Overnight, the snow disappeared and the migrating birds returned in overwhelming numbers, filling the once-frigid air with their songs. Well, perhaps that's a bit of an exaggeration, but it seemed so abrupt at the time. This year, spring is creeping in, slowly forcing its way through old man winter's clenched and gnarled hands. Yesterday, the cardinal sang for the first time since last summer; this morning, that bird and I awoke to a thermometer that read 18 degrees and there was a fresh dusting of snow. Even the robins and red-winged blackbirds are late in their return. I did see several sand cranes flying in slow formation yesterday; but unfortunately they were heading the wrong way.

I know that, slow or fast, spring will arrive. This event is an annual miracle that never ceases to amaze me. I am always in awe of the way various plants and animals survive the bitter cold. When it's late December and the wind is howling outside of my bedroom window, I find myself wondering where the sparrows are sleeping and how they manage to keep warm. They must welcome April's longer days and the warmth the sunlight has to offer. The brush in my field and along the roads is beginning to bud, but I have yet to see any sign of my tulips and daffodils. Their beds are now covered with a fresh blanket of the cold, white stuff.

Soon there will be a garden to till, new flowers to plant, and mosquitoes to swat. I have often jokingly said that Wisconsin has only three seasons–too hot, too cold, and too many bugs. But we're tough in this part of the country, and we've learned to endure. If you're lucky (and smart) you'll have your raking done and at least some of your garden planted before the winged-pests arrive. They're annoying, but we've grown to accept them as just another part of the changing seasons in our small section of the world.

For me, the best part of this season is planting. I always know when spring is getting near because I get this overwhelming urge to plant trees. I plant them everywhere–you can do that when you're filling up several acres and landscaping a yard that used to be a hay field. There's just something magical about putting small seedlings in the ground and watching them grow. I'll admit that when it's July (and 90 degrees in the shade) and I'm scrambling to water them all for the third week in a row, I question the sanity of my planting urges. But years later, when I look up at them towering over me (and I'm short, so that doesn't take too long!) I know that there's magic in the world, and magic in life.

So I welcome spring with open arms. Its gift to us and to life is a promise of future seasons and new beginnings. It gives us a chance to throw open the windows, take a deep breath, and relish the thought that we've made it through yet another Wisconsin winter. Life is good and magic abounds. In fact, once you get past the mosquito season, it doesn't get any better than this!

Remembering Memorial Day

Well, the big weekend is over. How nice it was to have three days off of work–three days to do with as you pleased. Did you grill out with your friends and family? Did you go camping or tackle some project in the yard, or did you simply take it easy and enjoy the time off? It's far too easy to get caught up in the fabric of our own lives. Free time is so scarce and our schedules are so hectic that we live for a holiday, and that extra time away from the usual daily grind. But now that the weekend is behind us and we're stepping back into the race, I just wanted to take a moment and ask–how *did* you spend Memorial Day?

The first official Memorial Day was observed on May 30th, 1868, when General John Logan ordered that flowers be placed on the graves of both the Confederate and Union soldiers at Arlington National Cemetery. In 1971, the holiday was moved from the 30th of May to the last Monday of the month because Congress wished to incorporate it into a three day Federal holiday. Opponents of the change say that the true meaning of the holiday–which is to honor Americans who have died fighting for our country–is lost in the hubbub of an extended weekend. I believe there is more than a nugget of truth in that belief.

There are those in this great country who remember and still honor the day in a fitting manner. Since the late 1950's, on the Thursday before Memorial Day, the 1200 soldiers of the 3rd U.S. Infantry place small American flags at each of the more than 260,000 gravestones at Arlington National Cemetery. They then patrol the area 24 hours a day to make sure each flag remains standing. Of course, communities organize parades, but far too often the theme is not one of remembrance, but a commercial one.

As a country–and as individuals–we cannot afford to forget. It is just for that reason that we have a Memorial Day. We cannot forget the price tag that comes with being a free country. We cannot forget the sacrifice our soldiers–both living and dead–have paid to ensure our way of life. Even today, as the fighting continues, too many of us forget about their struggles because we're too concerned with our own struggles of getting to work and paying the bills. The war, and their role in it, seem very far away.

Memorial Day, 2003, is over. The grills have been cleaned, the guests have gone home, and most of us are back at work. The summer looms before us, the kids are anxious for school to let out and we're already looking forward to the Fourth of July. But our sons are still carrying weapons in a foreign land and sleeping on foreign soil. We pray for their safe return. But, until then, how dare we fail to remember?

Summertime

Roused from its sleep by a chorus of singing birds, the sun rises early–aware of everything that must be done today. It stretches warm, yet overpowering fingers across the land–hinting at the heat the day will bring. You pull the shades and close the windows, trying to lock it outside your door.

You turn on the sprinkler and mix lemonade. A whisper of a breeze stirs the clothes as you hang them out to dry. It is a good day to wash. Smiling, you look forward to the fresh smelling sheets that will wrap around you at the end of the day. Back inside, the soft hum of a fan murmurs as it oscillates its head back and forth, back and forth. It's not air conditioning, but it helps.

Too hot to cook, you make sandwiches and salads for lunch, with ice-cream sundaes to round out the meal. You are grateful calories don't count in the summer, and to celebrate you add an extra scoop. Outside your window, the world's gone hazy, trapped in a pocket of hot, humid air. You make a mental note to refill the birdbath before you water the garden, wind up the hose, and carry it in.

You walk out to get your mail. A mile or more away, a tractor and baler are gathering up the windrows of dried hay, food for another winter. The pitch of the laboring machines rise and fall in an exact rhythm–one a retired or has-been farmer will never forget. It is the sound of good, hard work, of storing away for the seasons ahead. It is the sound of a way of life. Still, you are glad it is not you on the wagon, loading and unloading the bales. Anxious to escape the heat, you step back inside.

By seven o'clock the house is unbearably warm. The drawn shades and closed windows could not hold back the heat forever. You wish you had a front porch, then opt to sit in a lawn chair on the grass. The air is cooling down, but you do not sit for long. It's not that you don't want to, but some small weeds are waving to you from the flowerbed–and a walk through the garden sounds better than just sitting. The birds are singing again, perhaps grateful the heat has subsided, or maybe they are tucking in their young for another summer's night. It's nearly dark when you head back inside. There's laundry to fold, and fresh sheets to spread on the beds.

Gardening Redefined

The gardening season is officially here! Gardening centers and local greenhouses are filled to the brim with flowers and plants of every size and color, just waiting for you to take them home. Perhaps you're in the market for tomato or pepper plants for the garden, or petunias to brighten the flowerbed along the walk. There are so many plants to choose from, and so little space and time.

I've been gardening for years–vegetables, flowers, trees, shrubs, you name it. I like to think of it as trying to steal my eleven acres back from Mother Nature, who seems to have her own plans where my yard is concerned. I plant perennials in assorted flower beds, and she spreads dandelions and willow brush as far as the eye can see. She even sends her deer and rabbits to help thin out my planting endeavors, but I persevere. I figure that, if I live to be one hundred and ten, I might just win the war.

Despite the challenges I've faced, the whole gardening experience has been a good teacher. As evidence of what I've learned over the decades, I am about to offer to you the true definitions of some very common gardening terms. They are not the same definitions that an encyclopedia or the local gardening center would give you (and for good reason), but they are accurate definitions nonetheless.

- Perennial–any plant that persists in living from year to year, especially if you don't want it to.

- Biennial–a flowering plant that grows through the first year, is meant to bloom the second year, but dies off over the first winter.

- Weed Killers–chemicals you can apply to your garden and flower beds to help reduce the number of weeds growing there. These chemicals normally have labels that list the weeds they are effective at killing. The problem with this is that weeds can't read and are thereby unsusceptible.

- Hoe–a tool used for loosening the soil and removing weeds from a garden row. Will also remove flower and vegetable plants, as well as any bare toes that happen to be in the way.

- Shovel–a tool that is a poor substitute for a hoe. Also capable of removing toes, it does a lousy job of removing small weeds from a row of flowers or vegetables, but is a great way to threaten quack grass and bull thistles.

- Blisters–rewards you receive for using hoes and shovels properly.

- Baling Twine–normally found on a farm, it has managed to migrate into the garden where it can be used to mark (then plant) a straight row the full length of any area. It can also hog-tie a 5 horsepower garden tiller in 7 seconds flat if you forget to remove it when you are done with the planting process.

- Stones–objects of various sizes, weights and outward appearance that are native to every garden plot. These can dull a hoe, break a shovel, and also effectively disable a tiller by wedging themselves in-between the rotating tines and the tiller's frame (if the baling twine didn't get to it first!). They make nice markers at the ends of the rows, and between different types of vegetables or flowers in the same row. Extremely hardy, they multiply over the years.

- Flower Bed–a plot of fertile ground where the family dog likes to sleep, and the family cats like to make regular 'deposits'. Also the only place in your yard where the grass not only grows, but remains green–even during a severe drought.

- Fertilizer–packaged and labeled chemicals that are meant to supply your garden with essential nutrients. Will kill if over-applied, become rock-hard if allowed to become damp, and is labeled with a series of numbers (like 5-10-5), which makes gardening easier for all devout mathematicians. The rest of us don't get it.

- Lawnmower–gas-powered invention that makes cutting your lawn faster and easier . . . when you can get it started. They are partial to the male gender and will start more readily for them (which means that they will never start if the man is away from home–especially for an extended period of time.) Make poor lawn decorations if left where they 'died' on a half-mowed lawn.

- Tiller–(see 'Baling Twine' and 'Stones'). Also another invention that only starts and runs when it wants to.

- Gas Can–container for fuel; usually found empty. Husbands sometimes fill these with a gas/oil mixture which, when fed to a non-two-cycle lawnmower, will cause the engine to produce a blue smokescreen while operating (possibly one of the reasons why the mower will not start at the next outing).

- 'Weed & Feed'–commercially-sold mixture designed to feed the lawn and kill all unwanted weeds at the same time. I have no experience with this item. I've examined my lawn closely, several times. If I used this stuff, I'm afraid that there'd be nothing left to mow.

September 15th, 2000

It is September 14th, 2000. The summer is nearly over. With a lazy stretch and a tired yawn, she steps aside to make room for another season. Like a playful child, autumn dances at her heels–frisky, and daring, and full of mischief. She races across the fields, painting vast areas of green with shades of gold and brown. She stirs the wind and chases the geese across the sky. With chilly fingers, she slows the crickets' songs, and ushers the robins and the killdeer on their way for their southern trek. Gone are the long, hot afternoons that lingered without end. It is a time to gather, and reap, and stow away for another time. It is time to take stock of a summer spent too soon.

Everyone I talk to of late is saying the same thing. We are still waiting for summer to arrive–how can it be done? It seems that the lazy days and carefree, summer moments have eluded us. We lost them, perhaps, in a race to keep up with self-imposed deadlines and goals that remain just out of reach. I know that's true for me. More and more, I find myself wishing that the phone wouldn't ring, for I haven't even got the time to answer it; or I wish that work would slow down, just so I could catch up with my cleaning and yard work. Play? Who's got time to play?! I find myself grateful if I manage to get the supper dishes done!

So, summer is gone and autumn is upon us–which, I hate to say–means that the holiday season cannot be far away. Have you bought all of your Halloween candy? It's out there, filling up the shelves in any store you go to. And there's Thanksgiving stuff popping up here and there as well. I think that the Hallmark store has had Christmas decorations out all summer! How can we even hope to slow down when the world is already at least two months ahead of us? Sure, we can refrain from joining the shopping craze and shop for the seasons as they get closer, but everything is pretty well picked over by the 'early birds' by that time.

So what are we to do? Like so many people I talk to, I wish the world would slow down, but I don't know how to make it happen. I want the summer to be as long as it was when I was six years old, and the holidays to be just as magical! I can't change the world and I can't alter time. The only thing I have any hope of changing is *me*. I will start by living in the moment and vowing to seize the day. Tomorrow I will notice how the goldenrod is unfurling its autumn dress, and how the heavy dew reflects the morning sun for a few hours longer. I will listen to the songs of those birds who will not sing for me again until spring, and I will enjoy the soft warmth of a favorite sweatshirt. I will live September 15th, 2000, like it will never come again–because it won't.

A New Month

It is officially October–the start of a brand new month. As of today, the year is three quarters of the way through. This month brings shorter days and brisk, lingering mornings. It is a time for birds to begin heading south to warmer climates, and for perennials to begin slowing their growth for their winter's rest. It is a time for putting on storm windows, stowing away the gardening tools, and arranging bright, orange pumpkins around tethered stalks of corn. It is a time for planting tulips and daffodils, or perhaps a tree or two, and a time for old, familiar sweatshirts and reflective autumn walks.

As of today, there are only eighty-five shopping days left until Christmas, and ninety-three days until the start of yet another year. At the end of this month, the sun will rise at 6:28 in the morning, and set at 4:44. Our daytime temperature will average a cool 50 degrees and overnight frost will be the norm. It is a month of change and transition. We close our windows, and decorate our houses, and unconsciously begin the vigil of waiting for spring.

I like this time of year. Sometime in the next few weeks, Mother Nature will force me to abandon the endless tasks of landscaping, painting and mowing the lawn. I will replace them with new distractions, for there are closets to be cleaned and an unfinished novel or two begging to be written. Indeed, unfinished chapters are already rolling around in my head. Through my window, I watch the colors change–or I hurry outside to witness a flock of geese passing over. I've seen them a hundred times, and still they thrill me–their voices crying out encouragement, one to the other. With a sense of humility at the greatness of the seasons, I welcome fall. I am warm, and cozy, and content to see summer draw to its close.

I hope your October is a peace-filled one. I hope you find–within its brisk air–a measure of true serenity, one that is enduring enough to take you through the hectic holiday season looming just ahead. I hope you find contentment in this changing season, and a deep sense that the really important things in life have already been taken care of. For you see, like the migrating birds and changing leaves, such things are resting in hands much larger than ours.

Happy Halloween!

The invasion is coming! Monsters and witches, goblins and spooks, RugRats and Pokemon will soon be all around us! They come in all shapes and sizes (though mostly small), and bring with them a voracious appetite–not for human flesh, but for candy! Yes, it must once again be that time of year–the one that we celebrate by dressing the children up in colorful, creative, or ghoulish costumes, then sending them forth upon the world. Let the 'trick or treating' begin!

From little on, I never understood this day. Even as a child, I can remember stumbling up to a neighbor's door, dressed in a costume that never quite fit. While my mother waited in the car, my sisters and I would knock loudly, then begin the wait that sometimes seemed to drag out for a week. We'd stand patiently in the cold, repeating the words 'trick or treat' in our minds, over and over again, just so we wouldn't forget to say them when the door finally opened. Even as a child, it didn't make much sense to me. I'd wonder why these people would opt to give me candy just because I'd dressed up and stood on their porch on the last day of October. Then, as now, I guess I just thought way too much.

I don't remember my brothers ever going along with us girls for the Halloween trip around the block. Perhaps they were too old, or maybe they were stuck doing barn chores. But my guess is that they weren't about to be caught dead in the same car with their camouflaged sisters. And we girls, with all the compassion of true siblings, were just grateful for the extra room in the back seat that their absence created!

But Halloween is much more than buckets of candy. Its history is rich and colorful. This night of celebration can be traced back to ancient Britain, Ireland and France. Back before Christian religion was embraced by the Celts who occupied these regions, the people turned to Druids for advice and leadership. The Druids were priests and prophets–very powerful leaders in their day. These 'priests' believed that the lord of the dead would bring forth evil spirits on Halloween, and that the spirits of the dead would return to visit their earthly homes on that night. The Celts would light great fires at dusk, in an attempt to ward off the unwelcome spirits. Tonight, those who opt not to be visited simply leave the outside light off, and the multitude of costumed creatures simply pass by.

However you choose to celebrate it, Halloween is many things. It is the end of another month and the beginning of shorter, winter days.

It is a chance for the children to dress up and walk through the leaves, in search of a house they haven't yet 'hit'. For me, it was always the night before something 'bigger and better', because the next day is my birthday! I got candy followed by presents! What holiday (besides Christmas) could be better than that? Honestly though, I think the scariest thing about this Halloween is the fact that it is an election year. Television and radio stations will soon have to find new ads to replace all the campaign ones. Sick of hearing about the elections? Take your kid trick or treating–it will be a nice break. If you don't have a kid, borrow one. There's nothing quite like children in costumes to take your mind off the really scary things in life!

Thanksgiving 2000

It's been a rough week. Too many hours at work, being pulled in too many different directions at the same time, too many bills and insufficient funds, too many things that needed to get done and simply no time to do them. I'm caught up in this huge struggle between time and commitments. To make matters worse, this type of week is becoming a 'normal' way of life for me–not an exception. And as I struggle to get a handle on all that I need to do, I am painfully aware that my only remaining child is fast growing up before my eyes.

And now come the holidays. I guess I've always been more of a Scrooge than an elf. The whole holiday season seems so commercialized! This year, I've even chosen to bow out of my family's traditional shopping spree on Black Friday (the day after Thanksgiving). I made an appointment to get the tires changed on my car instead. I simply refuse to fight those crowds for a few needed gifts. No one will ever convince me it's worth standing in a checkout line for forty minutes to get a 'good deal'. As Susan Powter says, "Let's stop the insanity!"

So I'm dealing with all this guilt–should be doing this, still haven't done that–and I tend to be too hard on myself. Wishing won't give me more hours in a day, and it won't make my children stay young any longer. It won't shorten my chore list, and it definitely won't help me get my house cleaned! The answers I'm searching for are really quite easy to find, but I'm too caught up in the rat race of life to believe in them.

So here's my official list–not of chores to do, but of what I have to be thankful for. This Thanksgiving I give thanks for:

*My family, who love me just for me (and that's not always easy!)

*My many friends, who are all as crazy and unique as they are loveable! I'd be lost without them.

*My home, despite the bills and responsibilities that tend to overwhelm me. I am truly blessed to have it.

*My many talents which challenge me and help me to grow.

*My pets, who ask for so little yet love me unconditionally.

*My job, which keeps my head above the water.

*Having a car that I can change the tires on!

*And last, but not least, I am thankful for my faith. I am beginning to see that, for the most part, what we do with Christmas (or our lives), is not what God intended. Some of us get the 'love' part right, but we forget what's really important. Let's cut back on the 'shopping' part of the holidays ahead, and concentrate more on the 'giving' part–not gifts necessarily, but ourselves. And while we're at it, let's remember to Whom we should always give thanks, not just on one designated day. For everything–from the daily sunrises, to the children and grandchildren we tuck into bed. If you're not including God in your life (everyday, not just on the holidays), then the biggest turkey is not the one on your Thanksgiving table!

Can Pumpkin Pies Get Carsick?

If I didn't look so much like my mother, there would be serious debate in my family over whether or not the stork dumped me down the wrong chimney. Never is this more evident than during the holidays. I'm not like my siblings. They like getting together. I like staying home. They like the bustle and the interaction. I like my peace and quiet. They walk in the door at our parent's house, all smiles and full of good cheer; I slip in at the last possible minute, eat, then do my best to leave. I'm not totally hopeless, though. I do contribute something to the holiday meal. I'm entrusted with making the pumpkin pies.

Those who know my mother also know that she can't be outdone when it comes to cooking and baking. She lives in her kitchen and loves every minute of it. But with a family as large as ours, she often ends up roasting the largest turkey that got lifted with a crane off of the Butterball Turkey Ranch. This also means that her oven is quite full–thus, due to lack of room in her oven and the fact that I live only two miles away so the pies will still be warm when I arrive, the job of baking pies gets delegated to me.

There is an interesting dichotomy in my mother's and my baking styles. My mother keeps her baking flour in a five-gallon metal tin which she keeps stowed away in the bottom of her cupboard. I buy flour in the smallest bag I can find, and I make sure to check the expiration date. She goes through butter by the case and eggs by the dozens; I pull the faded egg cartons from the back of the frig and float each one before I use it. If they all float (meaning that their 'contents' are questionable), I actually consider myself lucky. Oh sure, I can't complete my recipe without eggs, but my tour of duty in the kitchen has just gotten cut short and I'm off the 'baking hook', at least until my next trip into town.

Of course, things are different on Thanksgiving morning. I handle my pie duty with a great air of responsibility. I buy fresh eggs and canned milk. The feast is traditionally held at my parents' at noon, so I am up early–stumbling about my kitchen as I mix up pie crusts. For the first few minutes, I think even my appliances are a bit confused by the flurry of activity. In the early years (I'm somewhat proud to say I've been doing this for more than fifteen years), I would time it just right. The pies practically went right from the oven to the car. That way, when everyone was done eating turkey, the pies were still warm where they sat, awaiting the attack. But my level of commitment has slipped in recent years. I no longer consider the timing to be that important. This last year, I even bought the pie crusts. Shame on me! But at two crusts on sale for $1.29–I can't make them for that! Besides, who would you rather have make *your* pie crusts, a woman who floats eggs or the Pillsbury Dough Boy? (I know there are no eggs in a pie crust, but you get my point.)

So, early on Thanksgiving Day, I am once again baking my pies. I am bustling about, completing the motions and feeling more than a little guilty that I don't enjoy this activity that gives meaning to my mother's very life. I even make a second dessert–a double-layer pumpkin creation complete with cream cheese and Cool Whip. Guilt is a great motivator. I begin to triple the recipe in hopes of feeding the small mob that is my family, but soon discover that I have only 'borrowed' two boxes of pudding from my mother. I shrug. Oh well, it'll have to do. The recipe calls for 'Half & Half', I use evaporated milk. It calls for the use of a wire whisk, I use my hand-held mixer set on low. My firm belief is that, if people don't like it, they don't have to eat it. It's not like there's going to be a shortage of food and everyone depends on having this second dessert!

As I am throwing this all together, experience has taught me to keep a keen eye on the pumpkin pies that are baking in the oven. My range is an old General Electric, I'm guessing from the mid-1950s. It's a lot like me. It does things its own way. Sometimes, when I'm trying to bake something at 325 degrees, it smugly thinks I am mistaken and compensates for my error by raising the temperature to 425. I really like that old thing. It has character!

All the while that I am doing this, I'm thinking to myself (shame on me again!) that my older sister is simply arranging vegetables and store-bought dip on a tray to bring with her from Green Bay. To make matters worse, this is the same sister who chose kitchen-duty daily while we were growing up, to avoid joining me out in the barn doing chores. She was always the 'domestic' one, and she's dumping baby carrots out of a bag while I'm desperately digging through my cupboard in search of the pumpkin pie spice I just bought last year. In her defense though, she does have Mom and Dad over to her house for Christmas dinner, so I'm off the hook for that one: not the rest of the family–or me–just Mom and Dad. But still, I don't have to bake any pies! I've often wondered why my sister doesn't bake the pies, being the domestic one and all. The only explanation I can come up with is that pumpkin pies get carsick if stuck on a vehicle floor for a distance of more than two or three miles. After all, Green Bay *is* 40+ miles away. Maybe that's why my sister really moved to the city!

In Honor of Thanksgiving

The best thing about Thanksgiving is that it is a time we've designated to reflect on our blessings. In all honesty, I try to do that on a daily basis, simply because noticing all of the good things around me makes my problems seem that much smaller. I do it a lot while I'm driving, I suppose because there are so many different things out there in the world to notice (and to be thankful for!) If I see a farmer out working in his field, I am grateful our country has land to work and families who are willing to do it. If someone is out decorating their yard, I am grateful that our country is healthy and prosperous enough to celebrate the seasons and look to the future. If I see a deer, or a pheasant, or some other creature, I am grateful that we still have areas for them to live in.

There really are many things that we need to be grateful for, and sometimes it's all in how you look at it. Two days ago, my son broke his elbow in gym class. It was serious enough to require surgery to reattach a piece of the bone that had splintered off. We struggled through the ordeal, one hour at a time, and I found myself grateful that it wasn't more serious. I was glad it was his elbow, and not his neck.

So, in honor of Thanksgiving, I've compiled a partial list of some of the things that I am thankful for. I hope your list is even longer.

I am thankful for:

- Courteous drivers
- My pets and family who love me
- No one flushing the toilet while I'm in the shower
- Hershey's chocolate
- My parents, who never stop being Mom and Dad
- My health
- The chance to get older and the wisdom that comes with it
- Baggy sweatpants, over-sized shirts, and floppy slippers
- That some of the Holsteins in our state still have their tails
- That I have a garage
- That my garage is actually clean enough to fit my car into it

- That my car isn't any bigger

- That I'm finally not afraid to be myself (i.e. crazy)

- That I'm not the one in charge of the big things in life–they still rest in the hands of God

- That I am in charge of the little things

- That I was fortunate enough to have been born a writer–for, because of that–I can experience anything, go anywhere, and fall in love for the first time over and over again, without ever leaving home

- That this list grows every day. Check back next year and we'll see what's new!

Happy Thanksgiving!

Christmas Procrastination

I haven't hung the Christmas lights;
they're still all packed away.
By the time I dig those boxes out,
it will be Christmas day.

And don't even ask about my tree;
let's skip the tree, I say!
The cats can't trash it–limb by limb–
while it's safely tucked away.

I haven't written Christmas cards;
there's no wreath on my door.
And I haven't started shopping yet,
that's what Christmas Eve is for!

I just don't want to decorate,
but my kids tell me I must.
It's so much work to deck the halls;
besides, I'll have to dust!

Am I a Scrooge? I guess I am,
but of this there is no doubt–
I won't have to pack it all away
if I never get it out!

Part 4: <u>Soapbox Time</u>

Cellular Phones–A Craze or Crazy?

I believe that a sure sign that you're getting old is that you can't keep up with the changing times. Take telephones, for example. I was impressed when they came out with touch-tone phones, especially the ones with the lighted buttons so you could dial at night in the dark without even getting out of bed. And the introduction of the cordless phone was great! I'm especially fond of the 'page' button on mine. That's the button on the cradle that you push when you can't remember where you last set the phone down. By doing this, the phone will beep and lead you to its hiding spot. Except mine only beeps three times, which isn't nearly long enough. So I usually end up pushing the page button several times before I actually locate the phone. On the first try, I determine whether I've left it in the basement or on the main floor. On the second endeavor, I can usually pinpoint which end of the house it's located in. Sometimes on the third try, I find it. It all depends on how fast I can run after pushing the button.

Then they came out with car phones. I was skeptical. And it didn't help that the reception faded in and out, depending on where you were driving. Some of them had to be plugged into the cigarette lighter of the car. They emitted a loud beep when activated, and again when you shut them off. In-between they crackled a lot. Personally, I wasn't impressed.

Now there are cellular and digital phones everywhere. You can't go to a store or drive down the street without seeing someone clutching one to his or her ear. Mothers have them. Teenagers have them. Everyone seems to be talking, and all at once. It's almost as though we've developed an insatiable need to be connected to another human being at all times, and our phones are our electronic umbilical cords. If we're running late, we can call. If plans get changed, we can call. If we forgot whatever it was that we were supposed to remember, we can call. We are never disconnected, never alone.

And these newer models are much more than phones. They can be used to go online and search the web. They have full-color screens and are capable of taking and sending digital pictures in a matter of seconds. If you're traveling, they can determine the best route. They can even provide you with the scores of your favorite sports team.

They can do it all, and still fit in the palm of your hand.

Of course, all of this comes with a price tag. Does anyone ever question what the driving force of the world might be if it wasn't money? I grew up using a black wall phone with a rotary dial. It was connected to a party line. One long ring told us the call was for the next house down the road. Two shorter rings meant we could answer it. It was understood that private lines were for the well-to-do and were generally considered a waste of money. Times have changed.

Personally, I don't have a cellular phone. I don't want to spend the money, and I certainly don't feel the need to be 'available' all the time. I have met my quota for distractions in my life, and my mind wanders enough when I'm driving and shopping without having to answer a phone. I suppose they're nice to have if you're running late or something urgent happens along the way, but experience has taught me that most problems can be dealt with when I get home. Hearing about them ten minutes sooner only robs me of ten more minutes of peace. Those minutes of ignorance can be priceless. I choose peace over paying for the airtime.

Too Many Cats

My daughters and I have too many cats. Too many, from a purely practical viewpoint, would probably be three or more per household. Two is a perfect number. With two, they have each other for companionship and the vet bills remain at a comfortable level. Despite being aware of this fact, our houses have more than two cats each.

There's a reason for this, and it's not that we're stupid. It's not that we're irresponsible, either. All of our cats are spayed or neutered and they're current on their vaccinations. We have too many cats because of other people. Our vet bills are high and our houses are overflowing because too many people toss animals out on the side of the road to fend for themselves.

Last fall, I had two newcomers join my household. I found Shaggy in September. I was driving home from visiting the Town and Country Veterinary Clinic in Marinette (a trip I am all too familiar with) when I saw something lying on the road up ahead. As I got closer, I could tell it was a young cat that someone had run over. The thing that grabbed my heart was this–its orange-colored brother was lying next to it, snuggled tightly against the body. Each time a car approached, the frightened animal ran into the ditch to hide, but came back out when he felt it was safe. As I had my dogs in the van with me, I ran them home, then returned to look for survivors. Of the two kittens who were still in the area–the orange one and a black and white sibling–I could only catch the first one. No amount of food in any flavor would coax the second one within reach. To this day, I still wonder what became of it.

A month later, a slightly-younger kitten came wandering up my quarter-mile driveway. We named him Snooky, and came to believe that fate had sent him. He gave Shaggy a new playmate and the two are now inseparable. Last spring, a tomcat showed up on my deck. As my cats are all fixed, I was confident he wasn't looking for entertainment. When several weeks passed and he was still hanging out, he gradually worked his way into the collection. Last week I found another on the side of the road, bony and scared. I realize that this could go on forever, but what really bothers me is that, for every one I find and take in with a sigh, there are hundreds out there I will never see. For that reason, there are a few things I need to get off my chest. Here they are:

#1–It is never acceptable to toss animals out on the side of the road. People seem to believe that cats are natural hunters and that, as such, they can fend for themselves just fine. <u>Wrong!</u> Cats are domesticated animals. We made them what they are today. They look to us for food, shelter, respect, companionship and compassion. They cannot survive in the wild. That is no longer where they belong.

#2–It is also not acceptable to drop them off at the nearest farm. Again, people have a perception that cats have this pampered life on the farm. After all, they get warm, fresh milk to drink and there are plenty of mice to catch. What could be better? The correct answer is–an animal shelter. For one thing, most farms have all the cats they need. If they don't, there's a good reason why. Cats and kittens that have never been around cattle and farm equipment generally don't survive very long. In fact, most cats that are dropped off anywhere disappear after a short time. Cats tend to bond to the place they are familiar with and will often try to find their way 'home'.

#3–Cats should not be left outside year round unless they have someplace to go where there is heat and shelter. A barn full of livestock can be a warm and cozy place, if that is what your cats are accustomed to. On the other hand, an empty barn, garage or woodshed provides shelter from the wind and snow, but little else. Temperatures in these places are far too cold to tolerate. Where water dishes freeze solid in a matter of hours, that's no place for a domestic animal to call home. Also, the notion that 'barn' cats (or outdoor cats) shouldn't be fed is ridiculous! People seem to believe that, if they feed them, the cats won't be hungry and, therefore, won't hunt. Cats hunt because it's natural for them to hunt, and some are better at it than others. I have three excellent hunters. They have all the food they want and they still hunt. Whatever they catch, they bring back to me. Yuk! By not feeding outdoor cats, the good ones hunt out of desperation and the unskilled ones perish. Providing food is not treating them extravagantly–it is simply the humane thing to do.

#4–It is not okay to destroy unwanted litters of puppies and kittens–year after year–and tell yourself that it's a better alternative than overpopulation. As a child I knew of a family that tossed their puppies into a burlap sack, complete with a rock, and dropped it into the pond behind their barn. They did this twice a year. No one in the family thought it was any big deal. I was only six or seven. I wasn't allowed an opinion. Well, I have one now. Such acts are barbaric! A family of four could go out for a meal at a restaurant and a movie and, in one night, spend what it would cost to get their female dog or cat spayed. Some people spend that kind of money in a tavern in one weekend and think nothing of it. I really don't think that 'cost' is the real issue–responsibility is. If you acquire a pet that you know you'll never use for breeding purposes, get it fixed. Period–no excuses. If it's a male, don't feel that it's the 'next guy's', or your neighbor's sole responsibility to have their female 'taken care of'. If it's your animal that's the female, don't just tie it up when it's in heat, or lock it in the house and think it won't get out. That doesn't work.

As I write this, it is storming outside. The wind is twisting in the trees and it's been raining for hours. My latest stray, Hoiam (an acronym for He's One In A Million), has found me at the computer and is curled up, asleep in my lap. I play hunt and peck on the keys using one hand and slowly stroke him with the other. I can feel his bones beneath his soft fur. In an ideal world, there would be a lap for every cat and a home for every pet. Until then I will never be able to understand how anyone could throw a living creature away.

The Right to Bear Arms

There has been much debate as of late on this old issue. That issue is whether or not people have the right to carry a concealed weapon–namely, a handgun. Some people feel that it is their right to do so; people on the opposite side of the issue aren't comfortable with that thought. Those in favor of carrying concealed handguns feel that doing so will make them safer in an increasingly more-violent world. After all, they argue, if it is illegal to carry an 'out of sight' gun, then the only people doing so will be criminals–which puts law-abiding citizens at a distinct disadvantage. On the other hand, people opposing the legalization of 'packing a weapon' feel that having more guns floating around will only add to the problem of uncontrolled violence.

To be honest, I'm riding the fence on this one. I admit to not having all of the information, but that has never stopped me (or anyone else) from forming an opinion. We base our opinions on what we know and what we've experienced. For example, two weeks ago this newspaper ran an article reporting that two juveniles had been caught destroying property. It would seem they had some fun by trespassing onto private land, where they shot up vehicles and other items using semi-automatic rifles. Hello! We live in a county comprised mainly of farms and open fields–not gang-infested, city streets. Was this incident proof that there are already enough (if not too many) guns in our midst? Maybe or maybe not, but it is definitely proof that there is a lack of control where guns are concerned. The youths used rifles to do the damage, which probably wouldn't fall under the 'concealed weapon' category anyway, but the report does make a person wonder just how many guns are out there and exactly who has them.

My limited understanding of this issue is that, in order to carry a concealed weapon, you'd first have to obtain a permit to do so. This would require an extensive background check, which would ensure–as much as possible–that you would not pose a threat to society by being armed. Laws and permits, however, are not cure-alls for any given situation. In fact, we currently have laws on the books pertaining to firearms that hardly anyone is aware of. For example, back in the 1970s, someone in Addison, IL, learned that there was law in his state that made it perfectly legal to carry a gun, as long as it was in plain view in a holster strapped to your side. So he did. He was promptly arrested, then quickly released. It would seem that no one on the police force was aware that the law even existed. And what about that permit; would obtaining one really ensure the safety of those around us? Would "George", who lives an honest life and obtains his permit with flying colors, then suddenly finds himself terminated from his job, audited by the IRS, and deserted by his wife (who leaves George to move in with his very best friend) still maintain his "low-risk" profile and should he really be packing a Colt 45?

I guess my point is this: we will never be able to control any situation to a point where we can guarantee, 100%, that it's safe. When you're debating the effects of too much chewing gum, that's not a big deal; but we're talking about weapons. Would I personally feel threatened if honest people were carrying concealed handguns? Probably not. My concern would lie in who's to say who's honest. The guns are already out there, whether or not you can see them.

$1 Worth of Peace of Mind

I mailed a package to my out-of-state sister the other day. The postal worker weighed the parcel and quoted me several prices, depending on whether I wanted it sent Overnight Express, First Class, or simply sent at the standard rate. I assured her that First Class would be fine and proceeded to count out the money. It was then that she asked if I would like to insure the package for guaranteed delivery. The cost would be less than $1. I smiled and thanked her for offering the service, but told her that I would rely on faith that it would get there.

It wasn't until I'd left the Post Office and was driving away that the irony of her question hit me. It seemed to boil down to this–I'd paid a fee to have a package delivered. For an additional fee, I would be *guaranteed* that the package would actually be delivered. What do they have, a secret room in the back of each post office where they hold the uninsured packages hostage?

"Here's another one, Harry. El-Cheapo didn't want to cough up the buck to make sure this thing got delivered, so screw him. It ain't going nowhere."

"Yeah, Sam. I know what you mean. Just toss it in with the others, but watch out–that package wrapped in the Piggly Wiggly bag has been trying to escape for days."

"Gotcha. Don't worry, it ain't getting past me. None of these babies are going anywhere!"

I continued to toy with the idea of ensuring that a service–once paid for–is actually performed. Imagine going to a dry-cleaning establishment and paying $15 to have a suit cleaned, then be asked if you wanted to pay an additional $2 to be guaranteed that the suit was really cleaned, rather than simply lost. Or how's this–for an additional $2 'insurance fee', the local grocer would guarantee that 'locally grown' produce really was; and for a $3 surcharge, you would be assured that your coffee actually *was* grown in Columbia, and it was picked by a man and his cute little mule.

Don't get me wrong, I'm not trying to pick on the postal service. Not really. I guess that, in a world of uncertainties, we are all looking for guarantees. How comforting it would be if everything was as it appeared–or as it was promised to be. What would the world be like if all of the popcorn in the bag popped, if all cut roses opened before they wilted, if all strangers were simply ordinary people we had not yet met.

Guarantees, like all things in life, come in various sizes and shapes–from little promises to life-changing assurances. In my life, I like to compare guarantees to chocolate bars. If I'm going to get one, I want it to be a big one–one that really counts! Go ahead, guarantee me that the world is becoming a better place; that we're finally catching on and heading in the right direction. Promise me that, someday, there will be no prejudice, or hate, or killing in this world. But until then, all packages that are paid for should simply be delivered.

Joe Joe

A friend of mine buried her family's cat last weekend. For twelve years, this animal had shared their home and felt safe in their company. For over a decade, it had wandered through their rooms and watched the children grow. For the span of its lifetime, they were all it knew. Now, no more.

It was not a young cat by any stretch of the imagination, but death is not something we are good at preparing for–and especially not in a case such as this. You see, Joe Joe wasn't ill. After twelve years, you would think failing health would have claimed him, but it never got the chance. Joe Joe was just in the wrong place at a very bad time. It seems some 'kids' who use a cabin down the road from my friend's house were up from Green Bay for the weekend. Out joyriding, they saw the cat crossing the road and thought it would be fun to run it down. When that did not prove entertaining enough, they proceeded to drive over the dead animal repeatedly until there was little left of something that was priceless–something that was loved.

So Joe Joe is no more. The sad part is, some people who read that will laugh, or ask 'So what?' Some will say, 'It was just a cat.' Nothing that is loved can be labeled with the word 'just'. It is not fair to say, 'It was just a doll . . .just a house . . . just a dream . . . just a dog'. Not if it was loved. Once something is loved, by anyone–great or small–it is valued beyond its measure. 'Kids' out joyriding who run down animals have never learned that. They have no means with which to put a value on what they've destroyed. There's a good chance they never will. That stupidity and their action–thoughtless and unspeakably cruel–have left a family to deal with the loss and the anguish. And the only guilt present is that which is felt by the family members themselves–by my friend. 'What if I'd kept the cat in the house?' She blames herself. And the blame doubles the pain. All for the thrill of the moment in some young, narrow lives.

Companion animals, mostly dogs and cats, play a major part in families all across the country. Untold money and time are spent on them. They ease our pain, they share our joy, they trust us implicitly, they love us with no strings attached. They don't care if we're cranky, if we forgot to brush our teeth, if our hair is a mess. When we are sad, they seek us out and search our souls with their gentle, questioning eyes. Their devotion is unwavering, their loyalty beyond reproach. They are, in a nutshell, everything we ourselves should be. They are loved . . . They are priceless . . .

I remember back in high school I had a discussion with my history teacher on whether or not animals go to heaven. As with all good debates, there was no winner or loser–only an exchange of opinions aimed at generating ideas. It took up the whole class period. Neither Mr. Graff, nor myself, gave in. He maintained they had no souls. I had no proof, one way or the other. Looking back now, it seems more clear. Perhaps, if they don't, it is only because they would have no sins to record there–and the only requirement they must meet to gain entry into heaven is one simple condition. They must have been loved. The Joe Joe's in our lives deserve no less.

A Lost Dog

On Sunday afternoon I looked out my living room window and noticed a small shape moving through the woods behind my house. Although I could tell it was a dog, it looked like little more than a white apparition slowly making its way through the brush. It paused at every obstacle; branches were hard for it to comprehend, as though someone had set down a fence to block its path. Full-grown trees towered over it, requiring the animal to detour around them. It hesitated at each one and looked off into the distance, as though it was searching for an easier way. When it continued on, its steps were slow and painful.

I grabbed a nylon leash and a handful of dog treats and headed out. The creek that runs through my land acted as a barrier. The small dog moved away from me, scared and uncertain, but ultimately it gave up. It seemed to be more afraid of the rushing water than it was of me. Ultimately, too tired and weak to escape, it stretched out on its side on the forest floor and gave up.

I can't tell you what kind of dog it is. Even now, with the animal safely resting in my basement, its identity remains a mystery. It was wearing no collar when I found it, and it fought the leash when I fastened it around his neck. Not wanting to drag the dog from the woods, I tried to carry it–but it made a feeble attempt to grab at my hands as I took hold. Not wanting to get bit by an animal of which I knew nothing about, I finally wrapped the nylon lead around its muzzle so it couldn't bite and then proceeded to carry it out. It felt like a struggling collection of bones covered by matted hair.

I'll be honest with you. The last thing I need is another dog. I am hoping against the odds that someone who reads this article may know where this dog belongs. He is a small dog, maybe fifteen or twenty pounds. His hair is long and white, and he has black ears and a few black markings. The sad part is that this dog is old. He's had a life somewhere–with someone–and now he's lost and alone. In the days that have passed since finding him, I have come to the conclusion that he's deaf . . . and the cloudy covering on both his eyes tell me his sight is probably poor as well. I am thinking he might have gotten disoriented and wandered too far from his home, then couldn't find his way back. I am hoping someone is looking for him, because he's not ready to give up on life yet.

Ironically, I write the press releases for the Oconto Area Humane Society and Animal Shelter. That this dog ended up wandering into my life is proof that we need somewhere for stray and lost animals–somewhere where people and their pets can get reunited, or where new bonds can be formed. If this little dog is simply lost, it is indeed tragic–but if someone tossed him out on the side of the road because they no longer wanted to bother with him, then that's an even bigger tragedy. This dog, walking on stiff, tired legs, is a white shadow that now follows me around my basement–silently hoping I'll stop what I'm doing and scratch its ears yet one more time. It's a precious soul that doesn't understand what's happened or why it's here in this strange place. It only understands that it still needs to be loved. If you might know where this dog belongs, please call. I'm in the book.

Reality Shows

Okay, I admit it. I must be stupid–or at least way out of touch. Millions of Americans each week tune in to watch Survivor, and/or any of a handful of other so-called reality shows that are suddenly the latest craze. You have Survivor, The Mole, The Bachelor, The Great Race, Big Brother . . . and probably one or two others I've forgotten. Now I'll admit, I've never sat and watched an entire episode of any of them, but I have caught a few minutes here and there, as it seems the kind of shows *I* prefer always follow one of these. From what I've seen and heard, a group of chosen 'contestants' are stranded someplace desolate and secluded. Ratings prove that viewers like to see the action unfold on an island somewhere–with sand, surf and balmy breezes. The 'contestants' then have to face an assortment of challenges (i.e. work together as a team, go hungry, find items, spear fish with sticks) in order to stay alive. And they each have to avoid getting 'voted off' the show by the other, for only the last person remaining gets the money–which I believe is in the neighborhood of $1 million. Oh yes, and all the while this is going on, cameras 'inconspicuously' follow them around–but they 'forget' they're being filmed.

If my memory hasn't totally failed me, I believe in one of the early shows, the contestants were sitting around a bamboo table with dishes in front of them. In the dishes was an assortment of goodies–bugs, worms and 'monkey brains'. Really? I turned the channel. I didn't even want to see who ate what. I guess it comes down to, 'What will a person do for a shot at $1 million?' Living vicariously, the viewers put themselves in the contestants' shoes. Would they have passed that test? Eaten that bug? Survived that challenge? And of course, they all would have.

My response is "Who cares?" Obviously millions do, but I'm not one of them. For one thing, being deserted on a tropical island is no hardship. Send them to Siberia in winter with one sleeping bag for every three people–then you'll see some competition between them! For another thing, I find myself asking, "How is it that all those people aren't at work? Are they independently wealthy–or unemployable? Is this all they have to do with their time?" And of course, not being the trusting sort of person that I should be, I wonder what really happens when the cameras aren't rolling.

It has occurred to me that maybe this show appeals to viewers who have no real excitement in their own lives. I know that sounds harsh, and I'm bothered that it might be true. Are millions of us really that starved for excitement and challenges of our own? If we are, we're doing something wrong. There are a million things we can do other than watch *any* show (with the exception of Dr. Phil).

And finally, how in the world do they get away with calling these things 'reality' shows? There's nothing realistic about them. Maybe for the producers, the shows fall under the term 'reality' because there are no scripts, no rehearsing–or so we are led to believe. This is not reality. Reality is not watching teams on television rise to a new challenge every week–it is finding and embracing your own challenges. Reality is not witnessing how the show's teams interact–it is interacting with the teams in your own life. Reality is not playing some temporary game where you're asked to do stupid, unrealistic things in order to win money–it is playing a lifelong game, one where you're supposed to help everyone else to be a winner, each in their own way. Be a survivor–rise to the challenges and tests that come your way, make your own life a competition and play your hardest. No, you probably won't win that $1 million, but that doesn't mean you won't end up rich.

Campaign Farewell

Now that it's finally over, I've come to the conclusion that our lives should be run a little more like a presidential election year.

Think about it. For months before the big day, we are bombarded by information about the candidates–their so-called strengths and weaknesses, their beliefs and goals–we are 'told all' in the hope that we will make the right decision when we cast our vote. We have months to decide, and change our minds, and decide again. But once the vote is cast, it can't be undone–at least not for that term of office. The choice is made and life goes on. We can vote based on our political party, or we can vote based on reports and stories that were freed upon us in inundating waves. But either way, we vote and it is done.

Compare this to other choices we make in our lives. I, for one, am an expert procrastinator. I can put off making a choice forever. For instance, I'd like to scrub my carpets, but I can't decide 'when'. No weekend seems 'just right'. Either there's company coming, or it's too muddy outside and it will all get tracked in, or it's right between paydays and the funds just aren't there . . . I just can't decide 'when' I should do it. As a result, it doesn't get done.

I'd like an 'election day deadline' on all of the choices in my life. I'd like to be bombarded by all the info I need for each decision, followed by a deadline by which the decision has to be made. I'd like to be able to weigh the pros and cons of my choice, and eavesdrop on people discussing which choice is the best. I know this is crazy, comparing electing our country's leader to scrubbing my carpet, but at least once my rugs are clean I'll be able to enjoy the results! If the money and time spent on campaign issues were spent on teaching us how to better use *our* time, I think we'd all be a lot more productive. Without a doubt, we'd be much happier.

We can't put off electing a new president. Eventually, the campaigning must end and the votes must be cast–otherwise the debates and mudslinging would go on forever! And, while my carpet may well be caught up in an endless wait for the 'Rug Doctor' to arrive, other choices have deadlines. We make them everyday. What's for supper, what will I wear, can I afford to lend an ear when time is so precious and the hours so few? Daily choices affect our lives much more than a presidential vote can. There's no Congress to veto the casserole, and there's no Secret Service watching over my friend's broken heart. It's up to you and me to make this country work, not the president. Because, when all the campaigning is over and the 'best man' wins, he may well fall short of the person we thought we voted for. In fact, he may have no morals at all.

I'm not sure what I want to be when I grow up. That's another one of those decisions I haven't quite made, but I know that I don't want to be president. I'd rather make the most of my own little corner of the country. That's a pretty easy choice.

Political Letter to the Local Republican Party

Nov. 17, 2002

Dear Mr. O'Harrow:

Thank you for taking the time to read my article and to write to me concerning what it said. I don't know if you read all my articles, or if you only read this one due to its political title, but it's always good to know that someone is taking notice.

I enjoyed your letter but will have to decline as far as attending a meeting of the Oconto County Republican Party. It is not that I don't value what organizations do for this area–and this country–but I already have far too many irons in the fire.

I found it interesting that you stated that politics are a 'fascinating business,' especially seeing that the purpose of any business is to ultimately show a profit. You also mentioned that you wanted to 'demystify the political process' for me. I'll be the first to admit that my attitude where politics are concerned is not a good one, but I'm not entirely sure it's because I don't understand the process. I am disillusioned because money is the controlling factor–not ideals, goals or dreams. This country, in my opinion, no longer has a government 'of the people, for the people and by the people.' It is a government run by large businesses and big money. You could argue that businesses are comprised of people, but that is not entirely true. Never before has the American worker been treated more poorly by big business. Workers are little more than a commodity–a number–and they are replaced and cast aside with no consideration of length of employment or dedication to the company.

My fault, if it even is one, is that I am an idealist. Nothing in the political arena–or big business–seems to be based on honesty, integrity or respect. If our leaders cannot stand independently for an ideal without fear of alienating their 'backers', there's something wrong. And yes, we the people are at fault. Ultimately we voted them in. But people are fickle and publicity turns heads. There is no easy fix for any of it, but my prediction did ring true. The candidate who spent the most on his campaign is now in office. What I want to know, and deserve to know, is what kind of a leader will he be–and ultimately how much will I end up paying to 'support' him?

Sincerely,

Kathy Campshure

a.k.a. K. C. Berg

May the Best Candidate Win

I'll keep this brief. I hate politics. In fact, I'd rather visit my dentist for a root canal than listen to all of the election crap that's been on every TV and radio station for weeks. The candidates–all of them–don't even sound like people who are capable of holding public office. They sound like spoiled children brawling on the playground–each one trying to dig up more dirt on the opposition than the other. I, for one, am sick of it. And the really sad part is that it seems these politicians are only accountable for their actions at election time. If you believe all of the propaganda, we vote them into office and they do whatever they want from that point forward.

Somewhere between Lincoln and Kennedy, our government and our 'representatives' came to a fork in the road–and they went the wrong way. How often do we hear the words honesty, character, conscience, and compassion used in connection with politics? More often than not, the words that surface are corruption, cheating, and scandal. One has to ask, are integrity and politics incompatible? If you believe all of the ads that these candidates are paying the media to cram down our throats, they are.

Here's a revelation–politics should not be about money, but it is. Watch a state or national election. The candidate that 'wins' is often simply the one who has spent the most money convincing us that he/she is the best candidate for the job. Is it true, is the best candidate the one with the most billboards, TV spots, and radio ads? Will he/she really serve us better than the candidate who couldn't afford such a campaign? Should we, as a people, stop long enough to wonder why the 'established' politicians have the most money to waste (or is that invest?) on campaigning? In my opinion, every candidate should be limited to an equal amount of money to spend on attracting us voters. Call it a campaign allowance, if you will. Level the playing field, *then* see who wins.

I know it's wrong, but I won't be voting tonight. Voter apathy is a whole other issue, and a serious one. I realize that's it's my duty (and my privilege) to vote, but after all of the 'finger-pointing' and all of the slander, I really don't feel that any of the candidates are worthy of holding the office for which they ran. They are certainly not what I consider to be 'public servants', and to vote on the premise of keeping the worst candidate out of office (as opposed to getting the best one in) just doesn't make much sense.

My bet is that, when the counting and tabulating are all done, it will be the candidate who spent the most who will come out on top. Is that a good thing? For him/her it is. After all, we're talking about some high-paying positions. As for the rest of us, perhaps the best thing is that all of the campaigning will finally be over. Geez, then we can get on with all of the Christmas advertising.

Sometimes, you just can't win.

Part 5: Short Stories

Not for Sale

"How much will you take for that old mare?"

It was October and two men were going from farm to farm, buying up excess livestock. This farm would be their last stop before sundown and they were eager to increase their profit for the day. The old mare of which they were speaking was standing next to the barn, dozing in the autumn sunlight. They had knocked politely at the farmhouse door and, after greeting the old farmer with polished smiles and hearty handshakes, were now following him across the barnyard. The farmer offered no answer to their question, so they pressed on.

"They say hay will be in short supply this winter; too much rain in June. A horse of that size must eat a fair amount in a day's time."

"Got plenty of hay," the old farmer replied.

"Still, wouldn't it be wiser to feed it to your milk cows–or to that splendid team of draft horses you've got in the field along the road?"

"Got plenty of hay for them, too."

They were drawing near to the barn now and the men could critique the animal more closely.

"Her coat looks rough and her stomach is distended. Probably needs to be wormed. That costs money."

"Never wormed her before. She's done just fine."

"And her hooves look brittle. You could only ride her over soft ground or they'll likely split. There's nothing more useless than a lame horse."

"The farrier is comin' the end of the month."

The two men were not easily dissuaded. "What are you keeping her for–does she pull a wagon?"

"Nope. Hasn't worked in years."

The two men exchange a glance and a wink. "It's a might foolish to keep her then, isn't it? She's in fair condition; she'd fetch a fair price. Why don't you let us take her off your hands?"

"Sorry, she ain't for sale. Now if you'll excuse me, I got chores waitin'."

Empty-handed, the two men left.

The next day, the farmer's granddaughter came out for a visit and the pair decided to go into town. The old man lifted the small child onto the mare's back, then handed the little girl a length of rope he had tied to the mare's halter. The old horse stood there quietly while the farmer hitched up the team. While on the road to town, a covey of quail burst out from the tail grass, but the old mare paid them no mind. Dogs ran out to the road as they passed, barking and nipping at her heels, but the old mare held a steady pace. Closer to town, some young boys went galloping past, whipping their horses into a frenzied pace. The farmer had to hold tight on the reins to control the team, but the old mare only pricked her ears forward and watched them race past.

Once in town, they stopped at the general store. The little girl climbed down but stayed outside, talking to her mount. She chatted about the great adventures she and the old mare would have some day. They were going to win races, and slay dragons, and outrun all those nasty, stupid boys . . .

Grandpa listened quietly from inside the store, a light smile playing on his lips.

"I heard the dealers stopped by your place yesterday," the store clerk said. "I'm surprised to see you hung on to that old horse."

The farmer paid for his supplies and shrugged. "I tried darn hard to sell her, times being what they are, but it turned out they didn't have enough money to pay me what she's worth."

Back outside, the old man again lifted his granddaughter onto the slightly swayed back. The girl leaned forward and tried to wrap her tiny arms around the animal's neck.

"Someday," the little girl asked, her eyes pleading, the horse's mane hiding half her face, "can I buy her for my very own?"

"You got any money?" Grandpa looked stern. Business transactions had to be taken seriously.

The girl sat up and dug in her pocket, but the only thing she pulled out was a lint-covered piece of hard candy. As though she'd discovered a rare coin, she handed it to her grandfather.

"Sold," the old man said. He took the candy, then offered it to the horse, which lifted it from his palm with a velvet muzzle. "I reckon she'll hold onto that for us so we don't lose it."

"Wow!" The little girl's eyes were wide and filled with wonder. "You mean she's a bank, too?"

The grandpa climbed aboard the wagon and released the brake. Before clucking encouragement to the team, he smiled over at his granddaughter.

"I reckon," Grandpa said, "that she's whatever you believe her to be."

The Tree of Faith

"As for God," the large pine whispered in the twilight, "He moves the breezes that carry you through the sky, and He cradles your young in the palm of His hand." The sparrow, which had been listening intently, swooped down into the security of the great tree's branches and, so sheltered, drifted off to sleep. The sun slipped from the sky.

The next morning, a doe and her fawn rested beneath the pine's draping boughs. They came each day, seeking the security of the massive tree, and found its faith as well. For the tree whispered to them as they slept, telling them tales of grace and peace, and the unending power of God's love. When nightfall came, the pair wandered off, uncertain of the truth of what they'd been told, yet somehow stronger for having heard it.

So it had been for a great many years, and so it would be for years to come. Ever since the young pine had watched a mighty storm pass over and had heard the thundering voice of God in the wind–since all those years ago, the pine had been speaking to his fellow creatures with a quiet and gentle voice, telling them secrets they had never heard in other parts of the forest. There were hecklers and those who would not believe, but the pine would not be silenced. With every breeze that brushed against its needles, it spoke of God's great love. This morning was no different. With the dawn spreading across the sky and the day brand new, a magpie landed on an oak across the meadow and began his familiar taunting.

"I am sick of listening to you, old one. For years, you've told the same, tired stories. There is no God; he doesn't care."

"But He does."

"How would you know, old one? You're just a tree–a piece of rotting wood stuck in the ground. I have flown far and wide, and have seen all there is to see. I have seen nothing of your God. So stop with your stupid tales and let the forest be still once more."

"But, I cannot be still. It was by God's hand, gently stirring in my branches, that I first learned to speak. To not tell of His glory would not be right–"

"Right? You cannot speak of 'rights'. Who are you, old tree, to even think of preaching to the rest of us? You, more so than all the creatures in the forest, have no right to speak of 'God.' Don't you know? Crucified on wood, His Son was; nailed to one of your kind!

And now you have the audacity to stand there and preach? Hypocrisy, it is–sheer hypocrisy!"

Then the magpie was off, anxious to spread his stash of trouble somewhere further on. The old tree fell silent, pondering the words of the ill-tempered bird. The hours slipped by as the hot July sun slowly worked its way across the sky. When evening pressed down on the forest, storm clouds were gathering in the west and still the great tree had not spoken. A myriad of creatures passed close by, listening, but an eerie silence was all they heard.

The great tree was still standing, very much alone with its fear and doubt, and still very silent when the storm hit. Even its stoic faith seemed to have deserted it as darkness floated in. The words of the magpie had struck the very heart of the pine, for there was a measure of truth in the bird's accusations.

What right have I, thought the old tree, *to believe that God is near? Why would He care for one such as me? The forest is filled with life far better than I. The bird was right; I am not worthy.*

The darkness had swelled, ominous and black, and the wind rose to fill it. It ripped the leaves from surrounding trees, and carried them off through the night. Brilliant flashes of lightning split the sky, and thunder shook the forest floor, and still the storm grew. Blustering gusts tore through the darkness, carrying shrieking demons of doubt and doom. They tore at the pine's ancient branches as they whistled through, and threatened to carry it away.

Sometime in the darkness, just before dawn, the great pine succumbed to the storm. With a loud crack, its massive trunk splintered and gave way; the tree twisted as it fell–down, down. In slow motion it toppled, its branches splitting as they struck the ground, driven downward by the tree's own mighty weight. A groan accompanied its descent–a waning plea in search of forgiveness. It fell silent as the tree stretched out along the dark, damp soil.

The forest creatures came in the morning, dazed and uncertain. They came to the spot where a chunk of bright, blue sky now replaced where–the very day before, and each day before that for as long as they had lived–familiar branches had offered shade. They did not recognize the great pine in its crumpled state; they only sensed something was different, very different indeed. Confused, they hesitated briefly, then moved on.

The pine was gone. It did not remember falling. There had been no pain as its massive length covered the land it had sheltered and loved for so long. Oddly, a strange peacefulness came over it. The constant weight of its branches, which it had hardly noticed before, was gone. Even its heart seemed lighter somehow, and the words of the magpie no longer mattered. For, even as the storm had wrenched it from the ground, God had caught the tree as it fell. The pine had cried out in its private shame, "Please, no. I am not worthy!"

God cradled it, whispering, "But, you are mine."

"No–don't; leave me be. I don't deserve Your kindness. You, above all others, know what I am. In the end, man nailed Your only Son–"

"Hush," God assured him and gently lowered the tree to the damp forest floor. "You are mine even so," He whispered again as He tucked the ancient spirit deep inside His heart. "Don't you understand?" His compassionate words echoed through the silent forest. "Yes, in the end, My Son was nailed to the wood of your kind. His blood flowed freely across your bark to mark His wounds and the cruelty of those who could not understand. But that is not what I remember the most. You cradled My child, and bore My beloved Son back to me. Come home, My child. I have waited for you through many seasons and countless years. You are weary and tired, and it's time to come home."

Conclusion

Mission Statement

It's a typical, hectic, Saturday morning. So far, I've done some errands in town, run to the local dump to get rid of the garbage and finished my dishes . . . and it's not yet 10 a.m. As I wipe off the kitchen counter, I ponder what to tackle next. The garden needs tilling and the lawn needs to be knocked down a few inches. There's furniture waiting on my upholstery business's 'to do' list, and some landscaping projects I've started that are waiting to be completed. And of course, it's Saturday–so I need to finish writing this week's article. As I'm trying to choose which task to tackle, the phone rings. Out of the blue, some very sweet lady is calling to tell me how much she enjoys my weekly write-ups in the paper. She tells me which ones were her favorites and why. We talk for only a few minutes, but it was one of those moments in life that make it all worthwhile.

I've gotten several calls and many comments about the articles over the past months. Some people want to know 'how' I do it; some want to know 'why'. Both are good questions, and both are hard to answer. I don't know 'how', but not knowing doesn't really bother me. I just love to write; I guess that helps. 'Why', to me, seems to be the real question.

In truth, there are many reasons 'why'. Some, admittedly, are selfish. I would be lying if I didn't admit that I would love to have my own column someday–one that I'd actually get paid for. To that end, having to submit these essays on a weekly basis to a small-town, no-name newspaper has forced me to discard the excuses of having no time to write, having no ideas, etc. It has forced me to just write. Who knows, when I have enough material I may compile it into a book and try to market it. These are pretty selfish reasons (if I were to be honest about it), but there's more to the 'why' part of it than that.

You see, I was–beyond the shadow of a doubt–John Denver's greatest fan. I have every album the man ever put out, some on multiple formats. I can hear your suppressed chuckles, but you have to understand; his outlooks on life and the world were very close to mine. He believed in treating the world–and each other–with respect. At one of his many concerts that I was lucky enough to attend, he stated that he hoped his music could, in some small way, bring people closer together. He believed that dream was a worthwhile cause in today's world. I agree. In the movie *Oh God*, which co-starred George Burns, he and 'God' had a conversation in John's bathroom. John was frustrated by the existence of suffering in the world, and he asked God why He permitted it. God's response was 'Why do *I* permit it? Why do *you* permit it?' John pleaded with Him, telling Him that we need help. God's reply was, 'That's why I gave you each other.' It makes sense, if you really think about it.

In some sense, my articles are shared in the hope that they will make you smile. I write about some stupid or frustrating things in my life, and people read the articles and tell me the same things have happened to them; I write about a passion, and others call to say they share it. The message is this—we are not so different after all. We don't all know each other, but our experiences—our joys and our pain—are one and the same. In many ways, we are tiny, individual boats drifting about on the sea of life. Sometimes, that sea grows stormy and we are caught up by waves that toss us about and threaten to drag us under—but all around us are other individual boats, and we can link up with them and find safety in numbers. It is as easy as sharing a smile or offering your hand; one kind word gives comfort to others in the storm, and that same kind word, upon its return, can bring you safely ashore. In a way, that's why I write. To make you smile, to touch your heart, to bring people together by showing them that they're not alone. In truth, we are never alone.

Made in the USA
Charleston, SC
05 January 2012